T0105807

Faces of Capitalism
and Socialism

What we know and what we think we know

John E. Jones

Order this book online at www.trafford.com
or email orders@trafford.com

Most Trafford titles are also available at major online book retailers.

© Copyright 2009 John E. Jones.
 Cover Design by Yang Yang & Weijing Gao
All rights reserved. No part of this publication may be reproduced, stored in a retrieval system, or
transmitted, in any form or by any means, electronic, mechanical, photocopying, recording, or
otherwise, without the written prior permission of the author.

Printed in Victoria, BC, Canada.

ISBN: 978-1-4269-0175-1

*Our mission is to efficiently provide the world's finest, most comprehensive book publishing
service, enabling every author to experience success. To find out how to publish your book, your
way, and have it available worldwide, visit us online at www.trafford.com*

Trafford rev. 12/04/09

 www.trafford.com

North America & international
toll-free: 1 888 232 4444 (USA & Canada)
phone: 250 383 6864 ♦ fax: 812 355 4082

To my wonderful wife Yang, and my readers

Chapter One

Introduction to
Faces of Capitalism and Socialism

Faces of Capitalism and Socialism is an attempt to simplify and correct false beliefs and prejudiced thinking about politics, in particular what the words Capitalism, Socialism, and democracy really mean. When we hear of branding and labelling we think of advertising, but branding and labelling are not limited to selling products; advertising and the media also influence our thinking about politics. Through repetition ideas and images become accepted as fact and the real meaning of words are changed. The faces of Capitalism and Socialism, and our perception of what these words really mean have changed dramatically during my lifetime particularly during the past thirty odd years. Other words such as liberty and freedom have also taken on new faces, and totally new meanings.

Since the power of advertising was discovered in 18th century Germany, the media has become the principal means of controlling people's thinking. Since the early twentieth century newspapers and radio were used for propaganda to support political objectives just as effectively as advertising products. In the mid twentieth century the introduction of television opened the public up to a flood of information as well as entertainment, and became the sole source for news for most working people. In the early 1970s in Canada business interests concerned that the public had too much influence on government launched a media campaign to change people's ideology1. In 1976 first Thatcher in Britain, and then Reagan in the

US ushered in the neo-liberal era that among other things led to giant monopolies by corporations of newspapers, radio, television, and movies. Public broadcasting has been reduced to relying on corporate news conglomerates for much of the news, and programming it presents.

The loss of any significant public and independent news sources that has developed leaves people with only a one sided presentation of world events of interest to the owners and more often than not ignores any stories not in their interests. The relentless advertising campaigns by business interests flooding the media since the early 1970s have been an effective propaganda campaign in manufacturing consent for neo-liberalism and free trade2. Paid advertising is a hundred percent tax deductible expense so it really costs the corporations nothing to promote their right wing agenda while the left supported by working people can not compete in the multi million dollar propaganda war. The result of all this propaganda is the false assumption particularly by younger generations that capitalism is a necessary or desirable part of their lives.

The development of the internet during the last two decades opened up many opportunities for people with access to the net and the time, to obtain the real news free of paid political propaganda. Today the real news or both sides of the story can be accessed through the internet and other countries are now providing news in English; however the number of people who have the time and computers to access all this material is very limited for many reasons and recent innovations such as face book and twitter have also been invaded by corporations and right wing paid bloggers. Never the less; the internet has been a life preserver for many people in remote areas of South America who have been able to alert the outside world on what is actually taking place3.

The most damaging result of the corporate takeover of the media is that our "representative" Liberal Democracies now represent corporate interests not the people, through propaganda, not an open forum. As capitalism developed into rule by corporate Interests representative democracy as it was commonly perceived ended4. When less than one percent of the population own most of the wealth and control the media, what else can be expected except serfdom

4

and slavery? Since the beginning of "free" trade and globalization most western governments following the US, and British models have relinquished almost all control over their governments in subservience to the interests of the capitalists who control most of the wealth and the corporations. The practice of holding elections is now just a media event to keep the public entertained and divided.

The meltdowns that we have experienced since corporations took control of governments, and devastated many countries; has produced a tide of revolution in support of direct democracy: real democracy by and for the people. This revolution began in the same South American countries where the will of corporations was first imposed with neo-liberalism; the latest stage of capitalism. Governments shackled with free trade agreements, the IMF, and the World Bank were completely at the mercy of corporations, and bankers. With their governments mired in debt, their social programs abolished, massive unemployment, and a complete lack of faith in the system, the people said enough already.

The commercial media in North America has been doing everything in its power to prevent people from learning the real news about democracy and what has been taking place in South America with smear campaigns, and or simply not reporting what is taking place.

The collapse of capitalism as a monetary system really began several decades ago, and as the cuts to social programs progressed mass demonstrations began in Europe protesting against neo-liberalism, globalization, and their tools the IMF and World Bank. It took awhile for North Americans to realize what was going on because of the commercial media but then the Battle of Seattle, and Quebec City protests took place. These were the first and last big protests in North America, but much larger protests had been taking place in European countries where millions of people at a time were protesting but these massive demonstrations went almost totally unreported in North America.

The protest movement in North America started later and was quickly brought to a sudden halt by the infamous and very timely nine eleven attack. Dissent against capitalisms neo-liberalism was banned as unpatriotic in the US following nine eleven5, and protests were also tightly controlled in both Canada and the US. South America was a different story where the people were just beginning to regain control of their governments, and beginning to build a new democratic form of Socialism for the 21st century.

Since 1998 following Venezuela one country after another in South America have elected Socialist leaning governments, and begun throwing off the yoke of the IMF; Oligarchs and foreign owned and controlled corporations and media. The revolt against neo-liberalism began in South America in the countries where neo-liberalism was first imposed in the world. As the people of Argentina, Chile, and Brazil began to realize that the IMF and corporations were controlling their government and reducing most of the population to serfdom they began to stage large scale peaceful protests that threatened to bring these countries to a complete state of economic collapse. Throughout South America people began to realize that massive peaceful protests and strikes were effective and that when opposing groups worked in solidarity they could even elect a government that would abolish neo-liberalism; and redirect the use of their natural resources so that they could be used to benefit the people instead of foreign interests, or enriching their Oligarchs.

A revolt by peasants against exploitation and expropriation of their land in Chiapas Mexico in 1994 had opened the eyes of people throughout Latin America that capitalism could be stopped. This revolt was the first against "free" trade agreements; the North American Free Trade Agreement; NAFTA that has caused so much damage to working people in Canada, and the U.S.. NAFTA was imposed on the peoples of Canada, the U.S., and Mexico, but only the people of Chiapas were ready to stand up and say no. People in Canada, the U.S. and much of Mexico sat back helplessly saying what can we do about it. Then the people of Canada and the U.S. sat back and watched the corporations move their factories and jobs to Mexico where the corporations could make more profit from cheaper labour, and lower taxes.

Capitalism in much of the world today is a dying ideology primarily as a result of the meltdown in 2008 caused by Wall Street fraud6. However it was the imposition of "free" trade agreements and globalization so that western corporations could own the world that began the downfall. The leading proponents of capitalism, the US and British governments are on the verge of bankruptcy; coupled with the growing reluctance of other countries to accept US dollars all Western Countries will continue to experience major problems. Capitalism traditionally provided a large middle class with a comfortable existence at the expense of the working class but the middle class has been shrinking and the growing working class is now experiencing mass homelessness and hunger. The huge expansion of wealth inequality has destroyed the American dream for most people7.

The US and Britain have turned to a reverse form of Socialism to protect the wealthy and their banks, but that was to be expected because they are the same people who own them. Unemployment continues to grow while state and city governments remain in the capitalist mode and are forced to cut services to the poor and growing numbers of millions of homeless people. Inequality has been increasing steadily since the 1970s in North America and Britain and bank meltdowns are accelerating the problems. The rich get richer and the poor get the shaft.

In contrast, in Socialist countries the economies are still growing; employment and social programs are on the rise and in former Communist countries where there were no homeless people and everyone had jobs and access to food and medical care people like Hungarians8, and the majority of East Germans today say they preferred living under Communism in the Soviet Union9.

The new Socialism for the 21st century that began in Venezuela enshrines the rights to healthcare, education, and direct democracy in their constitution. As knowledge of the New Socialism for the 21st century spread throughout South America it has obtained the support of the mass majority for obvious reasons. In 2009 an organization called ALBA formally became the new trading block for many left leaning governments in Latin America and will begin trading among themselves in 2010 with their own new currency called the Sucre.

Although it is not common knowledge yet, it must be very embarrassing for the US government that they can not provide universal health care for their people while socialist governments can and do, and not just for their own citizens. It is also not widely known that Socialist Venezuela has been subsidizing heating oil to poor people in 23 U.S. states10, and for subsidizing transportation for the poor in London England. This kind of behaviour is not acceptable to Capitalists; even more embarrassing for capitalists is the fact that real democracy has arrived in South America and it is spreading. Plans are already underway for a war against these upstart countries that are bringing real democracy to the people of South America to prevent it spreading north11.

In Communist Cuba today there are some people who are unhappy that they do not have all the toys and latest fashions and gadgets that are advertised through corporate capitalist media, but they all have a roof over their heads, food to eat, and one of the best medical and educational systems in the world. The global meltdown has had little impact on Cuba, and tourism their number two industry has continued to grow while it has been deteriorating in most western countries12. Cubans do not need two or three jobs or both parents working to support a family, they still enjoy the luxury of free time and a family life. How many people in North America would prefer the benefits of living in Cuba?

This is not to say that Communism is the best system in the world but the evidence says that it is far superior to Capitalism for the welfare of the entire population of a country instead of a privileged few, as we see in Capitalist countries. We need to understand what the word democracy really means and if it is possible to achieve it. The new attempts at Socialism hold great promise and only time will tell which model will be the best. Venezuela and China are the current leaders in attempting to develop a new kind of Socialism for the 21st century. China is moving through a peaceful revolution from Communism to Socialism by adopting a market economy with Chinese features. Venezuela is also undergoing a peaceful revolution but from capitalism to socialism, and a market economy, a much more difficult task. In both cases the encouragement and assistance to small businesses have been a driving force in their success, and key industries and their central banks are under public ownership.

As the meltdown of 2008 proceeded into the fall of 2009 it was obvious that Socialist countries were still raising their GNP and the standard of living of their people while Capitalist countries were still declining with no end in sight. The new socialism has a great deal in common with the development of the Canadian and US economies more than a century ago when mercantilism prevailed, private monopolies were illegal, the public owned the bank, and the government printed the money.

When Venezuela started down the road to socialism with Hugo Chavez he obtained Cuban teachers to educate the people and Cuban doctors and medical staff to provide medical care, and train Venezuelans. Venezuela was not the first South American country in history to adopt socialism; but it was the first to eradicate illiteracy, provide universal medical care, and food13. As socialism advanced to Bolivia and beyond the rights to education, healthcare, and food have been enshrined in their constitutions.

As Cuba had demonstrated half a century earlier, educating the people is the surest way to defeat capitalism. Following Venezuela's success other countries in South America elected Socialist leaning governments and educated their people for the first time in history also. These South American countries on the socialist path are uniting to defeat neo-liberalism, and US style globalization; most of them have refused to sign "free" trade agreements with the US and have been developing fair trade agreements that promote market economies and mercantilism around the world instead of predatory capitalism.

It is very easy to see by looking at statistics for various countries what is wrong with "free" trade and globalization. The US does not have universal health care and a large part of the population have no health care because they can't afford it. The US had a huge homeless population estimated in 2005 to be between 2.3 and 3.5 million14; a report in 2006 claimed that two of every hundred children were homeless in the US15. The US has the largest per capita prison population in the world which says a great deal about their rights and freedom16. Inequality in major US cities rivals Africa according to the UN17. The US has the poorest educational system of any industrialized first world country18. Slightly more than half of the registered voters in the US bother to cast a ballot which shows that nearly half the population realize that it makes no difference whether they vote for Capitalist party A or B; the corporations rule. A similar trend in the voting pattern has been developing in Canada for the same reasons. The corporate government solution in Australia for disbelieving voters was to fine everyone who did not cast a ballot but it also produced a lot of spoiled ballots and did nothing to convince Australians that they had a democratic government.

Crime runs amok in the U.S., and the capital city Washington DC has the distinction of being known as the murder capital of the world19. The crime situation in both the US and Canada has become so bad that we regularly have police shooting people and tasering them to death. Socialist China with four times the population of the U.S. has an unarmed police force; and one fifth as many people in prison. What is wrong with this picture? In Canada and U.S. cities we live with police sirens blaring day and night and helicopters disturbing our sleep. In China you never hear police sirens or helicopters thumping overhead conducting surveillance on the population. The population of Beijing China is over seventeen million and yet it is quieter, and safer than most large cities in North America.

How most of us have been so misled is really quite simple, we just don't know what is going on in the world20,21. A few wealthy capitalists have bought and monopolize most of the media in western countries and only publish or show news that is in their interests and propagate a great deal of misinformation and propaganda. The greatest obstacles to democracy are a lack of education and control of the media. Where corporate interests and Oligarchs control the government, the media publishes and broad-casts nothing that is not their interests. Likewise when the corporations gain control of a country usually through monopolies and "free" trade, corporate power and the IMF force privatization of education along with everything else that they can get away with; an uneducated and illiterate population, are gullible and most easily manipulated and controlled by corporate media.

Before we got free trade in Canada we had an excellent public broadcasting system the CBC, but since then it has suffered funding cuts on a regular basis to such an extent that it no longer is capable of investigative reporting; now it just relays international news provided by the corporate media. While I have kept the text of this book and simple I have provided many reference sites where real news may be found by anyone interested in pursuing any of the subject matter.

The turning point for our standard of living and the pauperization and or enslavement to debt of most of the working people living in North America and Britain began in the 1970s with Thatcher, and Reagan's neo-liberalism; it was spread to other countries in the world with "free" trade agreements advocating globalization that empowered corporations to rape and pillage all countries that were gullible enough to sign on. "Free" trade agreements were a passport for corporations to buy and control natural resources and relocate production to any country that would enable them to make a higher profit.

Globalization and "free" trade advocates failed to realize that when they exported the jobs of many highly paid workers they were destroying their domestic economies. People with limited or no income could no longer afford to buy the imported products and neither could the people producing them in the developing countries that were working for peanuts and struggling just to survive. Without a viable market the profitability of a corporation disappears and meltdowns and bankruptcies follow.

The quest for democracy and an egalitarian society has been going on for more than two thousand years. I have not found the answers or a solution but I have discovered that there are better options than what we have been putting up with, that there is hope for a better future without neo-liberal capitalismism.

Chapter Two

A brief History and outline of Capitalism, Socialism, Anarchy, and Islam

Capitalism and Socialism as ideologies have been around at least since the beginning of the industrialization of England, before the US was born, and are elements of almost all governments, in the world to some degree.

In the US capitalism is also the single ideology of the political system; and has become a culture.22 Personal democracy and freedoms are rights enshrined in constitutions to protect the people, and have nothing to do with Capitalism which primarily dictates monetary policies and protects corporations today.

In North America, people have been led, to believe, that Capitalism, US style, is the only system that guarantees democracy, and freedom; although nothing could be further from the truth. A century ago U.S. and Canadian socialist, communist, and anarchist workers were engaged in a constant battle against capitalists to establish unions so they could obtain reasonable working conditions and wages. A period of social democracy followed in which social programs were implemented, and people were allowed to form unions and obtain decent working conditions. In recent decades these advances have been reversed. The main sources of news media has been monopolised by a few corporations and recent generations have grown up bombarded and victimized by corporate capitalist propaganda.

In a Capitalistic society there can be no democracy; as Albert Einstein wrote in 1949: "… capitalists inevitably control, directly or indirectly, the main sources of information (press, radio, education)"23. People in the U.S. have been indoctrinated, to believe in capitalism from the time they begin to think, and talk, much the same, as people were taught to believe in various religions that controlled their lives throughout history. Capitalisms promotion of a consumer society is now seen by many as the chief cause of global warning, among other things. The global food shortage is also a product of capitalist drive for globalization with capitalist corporations controlling vast acreages in third world countries and using the land to produce a single crop for export, or to turn food into fuel depriving the people of land to grow their own food24.

Capitalists believe that they have a right to appropriate anything from the commons for their personal profit; land, natural resources, water, public utilities, media, education, and anything thing else that belongs to the public. The old belief that all men are born equal is just a myth to capitalists.

Trade, Mercantilism, Market, and Capitalist Economies.

International trade began even before the introduction of money in the form of gold or silver coins. In a free market economy peoples from different countries traded with out being taxed or regulated the same as they traded in their towns and cities at home. This basic form of trade is reappearing among a group of countries in South America in an organization called ALBA. Mercantilism appeared more than four hundred years ago as a tool for nationalism to facilitate exports and reduce imports through tariffs and taxes; the first features of what was later to become capitalism. Imperialism followed with the discovery of the new world and conquests around the globe by western powers building empires through military conquest. Modern Imperialism, capitalism seeks to do the same thing with money and the threat of force.

Capitalism today is also commonly referred to as a "Liberal Market Economy" or neo-liberalism, but in reality means capitalist owned or controlled labour, the means of production, and natural resources. Capitalism is both an economic system and a social system in the U.S.; although the US has some socialist programs such as social security and unemployment insurance. Most countries today have mixed market economies that contain varying elements of both capitalism and socialism. The failure of Russian communism, U.S., and British capitalism are all due to the lack of democracy; both became dictatorships of an elite group of power hungry individuals.

Socialism

Socialism has been traditionally portrayed in the US and more recently through out North America, as evil, or Communist; however programs such as public education, unemployment insurance, social security, and old pensions are basic socialist programs. Most Western European countries also have Socialist political parties that often hold power, usually in Coalition governments; and many countries have a number of different political ideological parties that provide a more democratic form of representative democracy. Strong left leaning or socialist governments usually have a national banking system, national industries such as steel, and control key natural resources such as oil and gas. In some Socialist countries public utilities, natural resources, as well as banks are also in the public sector, but this varies from one country to another.

In the mixed economies, of the G8, the US, is the only country without universal health care. Meanwhile the US has the most expensive health care system in the world, and 50 million people with no health care at all because their system is capitalist, private for profit.

Socialists define Capital as accumulated wealth, be it money, property or in kind, usually from the pursuit of profit generated by the labours of others, or from land, and national resources appropriated from common ownership; and used to produce more private profit and wealth. Karl Marx the father of Socialism predicted that capitalism would produce growing misery for workers as competition for profit led capitalists to adopt labour saving machinery, creating a "reserve army of the unemployed" who would eventually rise up and seize the means of production. This has begun to take place in several countries recently due to capitalists relocating their means of production to take advantage of cheaper labour.

The new socialism being implemented for the 21st century is an attempt to escape from capitalist imperialist ambitions to control their countries through international corporations, and "free" trade agreements. By re-nationalising their natural resources and nationalizing banks which are really the property of the people, the profits can be used to increase the standard of living for their people and provide social programs such as education, health care, and food. The New Socialism is also direct democracy placing the government under the control of the people instead of corporations, Oligarchs, or liberal democracies. The myth that people need bosses, owners, or capitalist investors in order to have satisfying and productive lives has been proven to be a myth25.

Venezuela is reported to have one of the most democratic governments in the world with a constitution written by and for the people26. Bolivia followed Venezuela writing a new constitution. The new Socialism in South America is strictly a non violent movement that has grown through mass peaceful protests, strikes, and blockades even when opposed by murderous regimes that beat, kill, and imprison people. The strictly pacifist movement and direct democracy are the most distinctive differences between the new socialism and the old model that thought only violent revolution would work.

Direct democracy requires that the country be governed from the bottom up, not from an elite top down model that has prevailed throughout modern history. The new socialism developing in South America places high priority on eradicating illiteracy; educating the population, providing medical services, food, and breaking the monopoly on the media by corporations; and empowering communities and regions to determine what kind, or if any industrial activity will be permitted in their area. Direct democracy from the local level as it is being developed in Venezuela is a feature that many socialists, anarchists, and greens support.

Anarchism

Anarchism like socialism is portrayed in North America as evil, and characterized by mayhem, and mindless destruction. In reality anarchism is egalitarian, socialist, and very democratic. The primary objective of anarchists is as little government as possible. There are anarchist groups that do resort to violence the same as capitalists, but most anarchists prefer peaceful protests. Many anarchists can be found working in food banks, soup kitchens, and various other community projects in Canada and the U.S..

Definitions:

Anarchism comes from the Greek words 'an' and 'archos', contrary to authority)
Anarchism is a political theory that aims to create a society without political, economic or social hierarchies.
It is both a theory and a practise of life.
Anarchists support real democracy: that is direct democracy.27
Anarchists advocate an egalitarian democratic society with no privileged class living off the labours of others; that all people not just men are really born equal that the land and natural resources belong to the people and can not be privately owned. Anarchism has much in common with the new socialism for the 21st century.

Anarchism is a political theory that governments are largely unnecessary and undesirable, and advocates a society based on voluntary cooperation and free association of individuals, groups, and cooperatives, organized democratically to produce egalitarianism.28 Anarchists believe in a society of individuals who enjoy complete economic freedom with minimal government control over the individual. Anarchists believe that public police forces are unnecessary in a society of equals, and that there could be no wars without governments.

Medieval Iceland illustrates a well-documented historical example of anarchism, how a stateless society and legal order worked with no government. Property in Iceland was privately owned, and laws were also enforced privately. Iceland was founded in 972, and collapsed in 1262, 290 years after it was founded due to a few people gaining control of most of the wealth; sound familiar. Ancient Athens succumbed to the same fate, as have numerous less democratic Republics such as Rome where the elites gained ownership of most of the land.

Less government is the primary goal of many Anarchists; anarchists realize that there must be some form of regulation in any society to protect the weaker members, but insist it must be done democratically. Reducing taxes and government control over many aspects of our lives is the primary objective of many Anarchists.

Reducing crime and taxes by legalizing drugs and prostitution is just one example of how this could be accomplished. Sex between consenting adults is really no one's business except the people involved. Women go into the sex trade for many different reasons. Some women are forced into the sex trade by pimps, which could be eliminated with legalisation. Perhaps most women who become prostitutes do so in order to support themselves or their habits; but some women simply enjoy sex, and having sex with different people. Some women like the big money, and the flexible working hours. Prostitution has been in the world since the beginning of recorded history and it is not going to go away despite government attempts to eliminate it. As long as prostitution continues to be treated as a crime women will continue to suffer and be abused, and the public will continue to be taxed to support the police, courts, and jails.

Properly licensed prostitution could contribute tax revenue for governments, cut down on sexually transmitted diseases, and substantially reduce crime, taxes, and the need for police. It is not necessary to reinvent the wheel or design experimental models. The US has had legal prostitution in the state of Nevada for many years; it has been legal in Europe for many years, and recently the country of New Zealand legalized prostitution29.

The same case can be made for legalizing drugs. There is no need for the open warfare by drug dealers and gangs on the streets of our cities; the innocent victims, or the tax burden for huge police funding to fight it. Following many years of trials supplying addicts with free drugs through their medical system the people of Switzerland in a referendum approved legalization30. The first benefits of this program were realized on the streets where drug related crime and violence almost disappeared. In dollars and cents the Swiss discovered that it was much cheaper to treat and supply their drug addicts through their health care system than it was to fund a war against drugs and the crime it produced. In August 2009 Mexico legalised drug use and not just marijuana31. The Canadian senate recommended the legalization of marijuana some years ago but the government caved in to threats from the US and has done nothing32.

The US tried prohibition of alcohol during the 1920s that proved that government could not control the production or use of alcohol but they continue to refuse to recognize that they are unable to control drugs either. Or perhaps they actually do and reap the profits. There have been many reports about US government involvement in the drug trade since the exposure of the U.S. CIA using drug sales to finance the overthrow of the government of Nicaragua33,34. It is relevant to note that Columbia where the US has been financing a war against drugs for years is the leading drug producer in South America. A similar situation exists in Afghanistan where the UN reported in 2001 that the Taliban had nearly wiped out opium production35, however since the US invasion drug production has increased very significantly36. Since the fall of the Taliban, Afghanistan's drug production has increased to and even surpassing Mujahadeen-era levels"37. A "Media Focus on CIA's Cocaine Links Is Long Overdue"38. Mexico, also under the thumb of the US has a murderous war going on for control of the drug trade. A US study endorsed by 350 economists including the late Milton Friedman found that legal regulation would save the U.S. $7.7 billion in enforcement costs and produce up to $6.2 billion in taxes39.

And then there is the matter of Coco Cola buying tons of brick cocoa leaf in South America, 220 tons in 2004,40. Coca Cola denies using the leaf in its' soft drinks so what does it do with hundreds of tons of coca brick? Coca Cola is the only company allowed to legally buy coca leaf in South America. What do they use it for? Surely not to produce cocaine?

Legalizing alcohol provided the US government with a very lucrative industry that created numerous tax paying jobs and a jackpot of new tax revenue from the brewers, retailers, and customers. The evils of alcohol have not disappeared but the gang warfare, and the costs to taxpayers to enforce prohibition evaporated; and revenue generated from the sale of alcohol more than pays for its misuse by taxing its' users. Alcohol prohibition was a no win situation for the US 41.

The ongoing attempts by government to control the people's choice of what drug they prefer to use to relax, or who they can have consenting sex with is futile42. It is time for governments to back off and give taxpayers a break. Prostitution and drugs should be legalized if for no other reason than that we could have safe streets again43. Lifting the tax burden from fighting losing wars; and making money from the drug and prostitution industries would take a big load off of the backs of tax payers.

Anarchy has a long history in Greece, perhaps because it was first conceived there; and Greek anarchists played a key role in defeating the Nazi occupation during the Second World War. Most recently serious rioting broke out in Greece in December of 2008 and quickly spread to other countries. The riots began with students protesting a police killing of a fifteen year old boy, but it was anarchists defending the protesters and attacking the police that sustained the rioting, and helped spread the protests to other countries.

Following nine eleven the US government clamped down on anti capitalist protests, and was followed by right wing governments in many other capitalist "democracies"; as a result anarchy has been growing underground and thriving. Anarchy is very popular in Greece today because the people have been victimized and brutally persecuted since the Second World War. When the right to dissent is denied, rebellion begins to form underground; and it has been growing in Greece for half a century. Greeks like South Americans clearly see capitalism as the enemy of freedom and the police as enforcers of capitalist dictatorship. Most of the fury that rocked Greece during December 2008 was aimed primarily at the police, and the government.

Anti capitalist persecution now treats protesters as terrorists in some countries and in Greece a number of people have been arrested, and are now awaiting trial under this new anti terrorism law.

When a peoples' right to protest against their rulers or government is made a criminal offence the only alternative left is revolution. Anarchists typically form in small groups, people who know and can trust each other, with little risk of infiltration by government spies. There are no leaders or organization that can be attacked, or coerced by governments Anarchists are led only by their philosophy that governments are unnecessary, and undesirable. Many small independent groups react en mass in major events because they act as free individuals in association with other free individuals in common causes. Common causes for anarchists are any anti government action; anti-capitalist, anti-globalization, pro-green technology, or pro-animal rights. Police killings of young people have drawn anarchists like moths to a flame and produced the most violent reactions, with attacks on police, and police stations.

Islam

Islam is the fastest growing religion in the world today and when we understand the economic and social benefits as opposed to the poverty, and ever growing inequality that has been produced by capitalism it is not difficult to understand the attraction of Islam.

Shariah law as it applies to economics appears to be the answer to the predatory, and unethical, capitalist practices that produced the global meltdown. Shariah law as it applies to the welfare of the people appears to enshrine all of the socialist ideals for a more egalitarian society free of hunger, homelessness, and the resulting crime.

Many people believe that if Wall Street had been subjected to Shariah financial law the meltdown never could have happened. With no derivatives, no short selling allowed, and no exposure to fluctuating interest rates allowed it appears that the meltdown could not have happened.

Islamic banking like the Islamic religion has been growing more popular in western countries including Canada, the US, Britain, and the EU. One does not have to be a Muslim in order to participate in Islamic banking and finance; like any other bank, Islamic banks cater to people of any faith. Shariah laws governed finance throughout most of the world for sixteen centuries, and people of all religions received equal treatment.

Islam and Capitalism have distinctively different monetary systems and standards for social justice. The feature most feared by Capitalists is that there is no income tax, only wealth is taxed. From ancient times religions founded on the bible and Buddhists have been forbidden to practice usury. Usury: the charging of interest is what propelled capitalism to become a widely accepted practice in many countries of the world although beyond the charging of interest there are many limitations when compared to the US.

Islam has rules regarding business that require compliance with Shariah law that forbid things seen as immoral such as investing in casinos, pornography and weapons of mass destruction44 The religious goal behind other restrictions is to achieve greater social justice by sharing risk and reward. Islamic finance prohibits people from selling what they don't own, which rules out short selling, and from engaging in contracts deemed to have excessive uncertainty on either side.

The Shariah stipulation banning interest is another threat to capitalism. Financing under Shariah law requires fixed tangible assets; no assets no credit. Most people who buy a house prefer the Shariah system of mortgaging because they know the total cost before they start and there no need to worry about interest rates changing or having to refinance. The title to the house remains with the lender until the house is paid for according to the agreed contract.

Paper money issued by Islamic banks must be guaranteed with gold or silver as was standard throughout the world until Reagan took the US dollar off the gold standard in the 1970s45. There has been doubt about the value of the US dollar ever since it was taken off the gold standard and as a result Islamic banking started to receive serious consideration as a safer alternative. Since 911 and the attacks and subsequent invasions of Afghanistan and Iraq, both Islamic religion and banking have really taken off; $200 billion was withdrawn by Arabs from US banks after 9/11 resulting in the formation of more Shariah banks46. Because Islam originated in the Arab world attacks against any Arab country are perceived as attacks against Islam and a threat to their culture.

Under Shariah law wealth should only be generated by legitimate trade and the investment of assets47. Many people have become very wealthy under Shariah law but they have done it ethically and honestly. It is still relatively easy to raise money under Shariah law for legitimate purposes. In September 2008 the Binladin Group raised $266 mn with a Islamic bond48.

Capitalism has traditionally been opposed by Muslims, as well as Anarchists, Socialists, and Communists because of the lack of social justice and democracy in the capitalist system. There are 1.3 billion Muslims in the world roughly a fifth of the world's population. Some live in quickly developing economies, some sit on vast oil wealth and some are newly middle-class Americans and Europeans. It is not only Muslims who are attracted to Shariah banking; in England where non Muslim people have access, many prefer Shariah banks. As Shariah banks spread into western countries and non Muslim populations gain access it is difficult to guess how many will seek this unique banking system that complies with Islamic law.

Since the meltdown of 2008 several countries have been scrambling to welcome Shariah compliant banks, such as Germany49, and France.

Chapter Three

The Progress of Humanity

In, a sketch for a historical picture of The Progress Of The Human Mind completed in 1794, Antoine-Nicolas De Condorcet speculated that through universal education, for both men and women, that superstition and religions would disappear and that war would be considered the greatest of crimes; through education great advances would be made in all the sciences and with new medical knowledge each generation would live longer lives, and that with industrialisation, working conditions would be greatly improved leading to more leisure time for self improvement and family life.50 For a couple of decades following WW2 Condorcet appeared to have been correct. In a direct democracy system of government such as has been developing in Venezuela for the past ten years, this appears to be a very real possibility.

During the first half of the 20th century, two world wars were fought, and people demanded change; Socialist, and anarchist principles including free education based on merit, unemployment insurance, and old age pensions became part of the constitutions of many Western European countries. After mid century the new effects of free universal education in the Western European countries could be seen in the world with the freedom of many former colonies, and a vast improvement in the standard of living for working people in industrialized countries. In the most progressive countries in Western Europe, free education based on merit became universal; superstition vanished, and the churches experienced a great loss of influence. It was easy to see that Condorcet had been right; superstition had been abolished, and religion had lost its' control, educated populations did not want their governments continuing to suppress other countries, nor did they want their money spent on military offensive capabilities. With the only the best minds being developed in their universities instead of only those who could afford to pay some countries such as Germany and France made great advances.

Religions still dictate life in many countries where the people have not yet been educated, and wars around the world appear to be unending. We now have wars on drugs, a war on terrorism, and revolt brewing as corporate greed systematically reduces most of the population to a subsistence level of living, and many to become homeless. Governments appear to be powerless to prevent shifting taxes from the wealthy, and corporations onto working people, reducing public programs, and giving away public property. Fewer and fewer people today in Western countries still believe that they live in a democracy; many people who lived in the former Soviet Union say that life was better there51. Communist regimes all provided their people with basic housing, food, and medical care.

Cuba stands as a glowing example to the world in improving the progress of mankind through education, health care, and feeding its' people; and in helping other countries provide healthcare and education. It was the success of the Cuban Revolution that inspired Hugo Chavez to take Fidel Castro as his mentor in leading Venezuela towards a 21st century socialism. Fifty years after the Cuban revolution the hopes and dreams of many people are finally being realised in Latin America. The spirit of Che Guevara, a leader of the Cuban revolution, who was hunted down and murdered on orders from the U.S. now burns stronger than ever and not just in South America but in Europe as well.

People are social beings who have banded together for mutual benefit since time immemorial. Society as we know it today would not exist if people had been antisocial. Social solidarity is a very common characteristic of people particularly when you look at natives, religions, unions, or women's rights groups. Each group works together toward a common cause or goal for the common good. The new socialism brings all these diverse groups together to work for the common good of all and since it is driven from the bottom up instead of top down as is capitalism, no privileged elite can emerge to control everything because democracy, the people are in control. Bur the new socialism is a culture and an economic system that has to be learned through practice.

Che Guevara attended the graduation of the first class of doctors after the Cuban revolution; none of these graduates wanted to go to the countryside they wanted to remain in the cities and enjoy a privileged life. Being a doctor himself and a socialist he had a different vision in mind for future graduates. Since the Cuban revolution Cuba has been training and sending thousands of doctors to many third world countries, and training students from many countries to become doctors. Cubans view medical services as a right, not a commodity. Cuba and Venezuela recently teamed up to train 100,000 more of these doctors during the next fifteen years. Che's vision has become a reality; this is just one feature of the New Socialism for the 21st Century52.

Is the path to the progress of humanity through capitalism or socialism? It is very difficult to find any signs that progress to humanity have been made through capitalist dominated governments during the last half century; the results have been quite the opposite. Not one single country in all of Latin America has obtained an educated population with out socialism, nor has ant Latin American country ever received universal health care with out socialism.

Education, healthcare, food, and democracy are prerequisites for the progress of humanity. Capitalism denies that education, healthcare, food, or democracy, are basic human rights; while socialists maintain that they are. Capitalism attempts to privatise these basic necessities for the exclusive benefit of capitalist profit limiting their availability to a privileged minority.

> "In contrast to that socialist triangle (social property, social production, and social needs), think about the capitalist triangle – (a) private ownership of the means of production and (b) exploitation of workers for (c) the drive for profits. Does anyone seriously think that this can be the path to human development53?"

> Michael A. Lebowitz.

Lebowitz concludes that to ensure overall human development our choice is clear: "socialism or barbarism".

Albert Einstein asked the question: "Why Socialism?54." In 1949. Einstein saw the relationship of the individual to society as the essence of the crises of the time in 1949. Has anything changed for the better? I don't think so. Einstein concluded his article for the first edition of Monthly Review in May 1949 with these comments.

> "Clarity about the aims and problems of socialism is of the greatest significance in our age of transition. Since, under present circumstances, free and unhindered discussion of these problems has come under a powerful taboo. I consider the foundation of this magazine to be an important public service"55.

Albert Einstein

In 1949 capitalism was benign and was just beginning to be accepted by many people in the Western World; but how its face has changed over the past six decades. The face of socialism has also undergone a transformation but much for the better. Today the taboo still exists in the corporate media but as in 1949 an alternate public media exists today and it is beginning to gain a much larger audience and greater participation. The old Socialism of the 19th century failed because it was a top down hierarchy that ruled over a demand economy; there was no democracy. Capitalism is a top down hierarchy ruling for personal profit and greed; there is also no democracy.

Chapter Four

Media and what we think we know.

Corporate media propaganda and the Search for the Truth

For those of us who live in North America, we have to become aware and begin to question why we believe what we take for granted as truth, who is feeding us the news, and if we want to learn what is really going on in the world we must look beyond the corporations to alternative independent media sources56. As Einstein pointed out, we will only get one side of the story living in a Capitalist system; capitalists do not publish anything that is not in their interest57. To accept any commercial media as true or unbiased is a big mistake considering who owns the commercial media and who can afford to promote their interests in it. The greatest enemy of freedom and democracy in North America today is commercial media.

A media propaganda campaign in Canada launched in the early 1970s by big business set up the Fraser Institute in BC in 1974 that smeared and discredited the provincial NDP party, eventually toppled the premier Dave Barrett, and neo-liberal government that resulted began privatizing everything in sight.

The "Fraser Institute was backed by a small group of powerful B.C. corporate executives, led by Pat Doyle of MacMillan Bloedel"58,59. Doyle envisaged as a "propaganda think tank to combat the B.C. socialists"60. The original director of the institute Michael Walker stated" "If you really want to change the world, you have to change the ideological fabric of the world"61,62. In 1997 the Fraser Institute backed by twenty five multinational corporations had a five year budget of $2.7 million dollars to promote economic freedom for corporations63. Economic freedom for corporations includes privatizing Medicare, education, and passing right to work laws to undermine and destroy unions64. The public does not have the funding or voice to combat capitalist corporate propaganda.

The C.D. Howe Institute established in 1958 had been highly respected because it supported a mixed bag of economic policies until the 1970s when it switched to supporting corporations due in a large part to relying on corporate sponsorship for funding. By 1981 the C.D.H.I. had shifted its support to the corporations and a bilateral "free" trade with the U.S. it had also identified the public as the most significant threat to corporate rule65; and later boasted of its success in converting federal ministers and senior bureaucrats to support "free" trade66,67. If a democratic referendum been held despite the corporate propaganda Canada would never had any "free" trade agreements, but that would have been democracy of the people.

The monopolization of news coverage by think tanks as compiled by Newswatch over a period of six months revealed that The Fraser Institute received 312 references, the C.D.H.I. 270 and the Canadian Centre for Alternatives the largest left wing think tank only 48. Final tally corporations 582, people oriented 48, a ridiculously one sided bias68. If people want to have democracy they need to look somewhere other than commercial media for their information, and if they want to discontinue being brainwashed they need to shut commercial media out of their lives.

The corporate media disinformation campaign is now focused on ridiculing left leaning Latin American countries and vilifying leaders such as Hugo Chavez of Venezuela who is establishing real democracy69,70. Democracy by the people eliminates corporate government so naturally it is the number one enemy of corporate media, and governments. Despite media reports to the contrary most socialist economies have continued to prosper and grow through out the meltdown while capitalist corporate governments were sinking in debt and their people losing jobs.

The western corporate media is global in its political propaganda and skewed reporting71. The coup in Honduras in June 2009 was condemned worldwide in almost every country except Canada and the US72. The only countries that did not refuse to acknowledge the coup regime and cut off financial and military aid were Canada and the US, but there was little mention of this in corporate North American news73. This coup was an almost an exact copy of the U. S. backed coup against Jaoa Goulart of Brazil in 196474, that spread beyond Brazil and destroyed several other democratic Latin American governments. Let's hope that pattern doesn't repeat again killing off thousands, and displacing millions of people.

The media spin in North America is the same old story. As in Venezuela in 2002 the coup in Honduras cut all news and even turned off the power to prevent people from finding out what was going on. The presidents were both kidnapped during the night and flown out of the country, and then the corporate media reported that they had resigned; bald faced lies. Three months later the media battle was still continuing over Honduras despite continuing huge public protests, repression, disappearances, murder, beatings and imprisonment75,76.

Canada's corporate prime minister signed a free trade agreement with Columbia; the largest drug producing country in the hemisphere77,78,79. Columbia also is one of the worst human rights offenders in the world with one of the most corrupt governments in the world80,81,82. What has our corporate media reported about these outrages; next to nothing, only the usual false reports of the benefits that are supposed to come to the people. The media situation in Columbia is even worse. The largest media conglomerate in Columbia RCN is owned by Ardila Lulle, who also owns three sugar mills accounting for a third of the countries sugar production; the national soft drink business, bottle making factories, and a number of textile manufacturing industries83.

The battle for public broadcasting space has been ongoing for more than ten tears in Venezuela where the privately owned media instigated a coup in 2002 now commonly referred to as the media coup84. In October 2008 Venezuela's president Chavez hailed the successful launch of his countries first satellite from China as "an act of liberation"85. The satellite was designed to offer radio, television and internet in three band frequencies and broadcast from Mexico to Chile and Argentina86.

The U.S. attempted to have China suspend the launch but the Chinese government said there was no reason to suspend it87. This action by the U.S. demonstrates the vital importance of controlling minds through the media. This is the first and only publicly owned satellite to serve Latin America and the Caribbean with public free speech. The satellite is also being used by the Bolivian government and president Evo Morales said: "I think this telecommunications satellite is a human right for the nations of South America and the Caribbean, and should not be a private enterprise88". For the great majority of people in Latin America this was their first access to national public media.

In the early the early years of the revolution in Venezuela the media was almost totally privately owned by the Oligarchs. It was a long hard battle to restore some of the air waves to public broadcasting. Hundreds of new local public media outlets have been opened in communities and are operated by community members since the corporate media coup against President Hugo Chavez. Avila TV a public Venezuelan channel now broadcasting from Caracas covers a much larger area than a community station and is one of several media projects started since the 2002 media coup. Avila TV now has a team of some 380 young people armed with video cameras roaming the city for news89. Avila started up in 2006 with 30 people and covers the underground culture of Caracas relating closely with young people. Avila accepts no paid advertising but does report international as well as local news, and produces its' own soap operas that document the reality of living in the city's slums that are very popular throughout Latin America90. The young Avila reporters have an aggressive style showing up with cameras and microphones at anti government marches, public restaurants, and airports searching for opportunities to confront opposition leaders and private media owners91. A second satellite is planned to be manufactured and launched for Venezuela from China in 2013.

Venezuela probably has the most democratic government and constitution in the world92. What does our corporate media report about democracy in Venezuela, and Bolivia? Nothing, and nothing is reported on the tremendous improvements to the quality of life of the people of Venezuela during the past ten years, only slanderous accusations and lies about President Hugo Chavez93. Our corporate governments are terrified of the new 21st century socialism rising in South America because it is democratic, and losing total control of the media compromises their ability to promote their propaganda. To have democracy everyone must have the right to speak and to be heard.

Having a public funded and operated station like the CBC in Canada, or the BBC in Britain is of little use to democracy when it is forced to parrot corporate news. Publicly owned media, operated and controlled by the people is the only way for the people to make their views known. Publicly owned and operated media in Venezuela is free of commercial advertising and that eliminates a lot of propaganda from various sources; like the Fraser Institute in Canada. Venezuela has a government station Channel 8 that is news based and government run, and this is fine for the government to promote its' news, and views about programs and policies with out having to pay private broadcasters. However government controlled media is not usually popular with much of the population, particularly young people.

In a democracy the people own and control the natural resources and the government; natural resources are nationalised and the profits are used to support social programs instead of enriching private interests; national banks eliminate the need to pay exorbitant interest payments to privately owned banks for public debt, and only the government is allowed to print money.

In a democracy the rights of natives are recognised, including their rights to land, language, culture, and political representation. Socialist China has 56 distinct cultures that have all been preserved and continue to flourish. It is hard to imagine what Canada or the U.S. would look like today if all the native cultures had been permitted to survive. Venezuela was the first country in the Americas to achieve a democratic constitution in the history of the Americas; a constitution written by and for the people and approved by a public referendum by the people. With democracy Bolivia was able to elect the first native president in the history of South America, and for the natives to participate in rewriting the countries constitution democratically94. The new democratic socialism is truly working in South America95.

There are two sides to every story or argument. Many countries today post news in English, on the web, and it is not difficult for anyone who has access to a computer to learn what is going on providing they take the time to search. Many countries as diverse as China, and Germany also have English language news sites and TV channels that broadcast twenty-four hours a day. News and TV from South America is now available but unfortunately for some of us it was still only in Spanish the last time I checked. As you will see if you look at the references for the information provided in this book there are many sources available in English to anyone who has access to a computer. However beware, corporations have moved to the internet too with everything from paid bloggers to corporate news sites.

Truly public news sites offer no paid advertising and articles are free to view free of charge; these sites are primarily supported by donations. narconews.com, venezuelanalysis.com. quotha.net, and zmag.org are excellent examples of well researched authoritative public news reports on central and south America. Canada's public broadcaster CBC was an excellent source for both sides of the story many years ago, but has been downsized and had funding cuts so many times that not much is left. Britain's BBC the public broadcaster occasionally carries news that doesn't appear in North America.

"Do you begin to see, then, what kind of world we are creating? It is the exact opposite of the stupid hedonistic Utopias that the old reformers imagined. A world of fear and treachery and torment, a world of trampling and being trampled upon, a world which will grow not less but more merciless as it refines itself. Progress in our world will be progress toward more pain."

George Orwell.

"In our age there is no such thing as 'keeping out of politics.' All issues are political issues, and politics itself is a mass of lies, evasions, folly, hatred and schizophrenia".

George Orwell.

Chapter Five

The Changing Face of Capitalism

During the 1950s a wise old farmer, my grandfather told me: "The capitalists create a war for every generation; stay on the land producing food so you won't be conscripted for cannon fodder." This wise old farmer wasn't a recent immigrant, be was from a Loyalist family who had come to Canada before English Canada had become a reality. Canada at that time was involved in a senseless war in Korea that accomplished nothing except an untold number of deaths, and helped a lot of capitalists in the arms industry get wealthier.

At the time the Korean War was regarded in Canada as a just United Nations intervention; not an attempt by the U.S. to gain a foothold on the Chinese border. When the U.S. made its' second attempt to reach the Chinese border alone in Vietnam it wasn't just stopped at the staring line as had happened in Korea, it suffered a crushing defeat and was evicted.

Capitalists had been recognised in Britain, and throughout the Commonwealth as the enemy of working people since the beginning of the industrial revolution a century earlier. After two World Wars this perception changed a great deal with the legalization of unions and implementation of social programs and for a couple of decades the life of the average worker was greatly improved. The socialists and communists were lulled into thinking that democratic socialism could work. The Big Three in Detroit with their well paid unionised workers were touted as the American dream come true.

In Canada during the late fifties and sixties a man could get married and raise a family with out a college education; or his wife having to go out and work. This did not require holding down two or three jobs; forty hours a week was par for the course; and he could buy and own his own home in twenty years. That is why many baby boomers are reported to be well off today.

The Evolution, Growth, and Downfall of Capitalism

International trade began in the world as a market economy that existed in the Islamic world for hundreds of years before it spread to Europe. The first development attributed to capitalism was the introduction of usury, or the charging of interest that had been forbidden in Islamic business. Wage labour began in Britain with the beginning of industrialisation, and the privatization of land and natural resources. Industrialisation made it possible for the feudal Lords to become Capitalists: the actual ownership of the country appeared to change however the wealth remained concentrated in the hands of the small elite with a few successful capitalists joining the ranks of the lords.

Clearing the serfs off of the land began with land enclosures to make room for sheep; the key to developing the cloth trade in wool. The eviction of the serfs from the land caused many problems, with crime, revolt, and rebellions that were put down brutally. When the prisons began to overflow, and the public was becoming increasingly volatile, the British Empire was at its' peak and the excess serfs were transported to the colonies in North America, Australia, and New Zealand. Former serfs made up the vast majority of the white population in these newly conquered lands and they certainly had no use or respect for capitalists or the British Oligarchs.

Those of us who have been here have witnessed great changes in the public's perception of our government and the state of our democracy among other things. Most of us used to think of capitalism simply as an economic system but capitalism was also a way of thinking in the U.S., and had become the culture. The American dream, to become wealthy and famous was capitalism.

Medieval Europeans introduced mercantilism, and economic terms still in use today such as tariff and traffic, originated from

Islamic business. In Europe, Mercantilism gradually evolved with industrialisation, into economic practices such as taxing imports and subsidizing exports to enrich the national treasury. Capitalism was basically a system that appropriated and concentrated the means of production: materials, land, and tools, as private property. This private property is called capital, and the owners of these means of production are called capitalists.

With industrialisation labour became a commodity, and the sole means of survival for most of the population as serfs were evicted from the land; as later the natives in the new world would have their land expropriated and become dependent on wages or the government for their survival. No longer being able to sustain them selves as they had since time immemorial, these people had no alternative except to become wage slaves, or live on reserves depending on government handouts. Under capitalists labour was increasingly made more efficient by the division of labour, in order to increase profits, as defined by productivity. The division of labour started long before the first assembly line in a factory, but the assembly line is a good example of the division of labour. Workers on an assembly line require very little education and almost anyone can be taught very quickly how to install one part into a car. Capitalists are very aware of the dangers in having a well educated population and also that only a basic education is required for most workers to perform their required task.

Capitalism as a way of thinking is fundamentally individualistic and selfish, that is the individual is the center of any capitalist endeavour. This idea originated from Enlightenment era concepts of individuality: that all individuals are different, that society is composed of individuals who pursue their own interests, and that individuals should be free to pursue their own interests. Capitalists call this economic freedom, that in a democratic sense, individuals pursuing their own interests would guarantee the interests of society as a whole.

However, as anyone can see, an individual Capitalist's interests, guarantee no ones interests except their own; they are antisocial. Why should a capitalist have the right to expropriate fish from the commons to private ownership and then employ a few of the former people whose livelihood and trade had depended on this fishery to work as wage slaves. The natives had managed the fishery for centuries as a communal endeavour that supported the entire community. What gives anyone the right to expropriate land or resources from the commons to fulfil their self interest? This is a matter of serious contention around the world today, and from Canada to the Amazon in our own hemisphere; as oil companies invade farms, and mining companies force people off their land.

Capitalists also believe that a bare subsistence wage is all that labour deserves, and that is all they should be paid. The result of the division of labour, lowered the value of the individual worker; creating immense social problems in Europe and North America during the nineteenth and early twentieth centuries. Following the two world wars social programs were implemented that provided a reasonable degree of egalitarianism and permitted working people to live a reasonably happy life working a forty hour week with good wages. Governments had little choice in the matter with returning veterans from the war making the demands and the rise of communism and socialism in Europe as well as at home. However since deregulation began in the 1970s, working people have lost most of the benefits of the social democratic programs and experienced a huge shift away from any reasonable degree of egalitarianism including the forty hour week.

The only goal of unregulated capitalism, cyber capitalism is to produce wealth, that is, to make individual Capitalists and corporations wealthier and more affluent than they would be otherwise. This economic growth has no prescribed end; the sole purpose is for individual capitalists and corporations, is to grow steadily wealthier, and more powerful. Of what use is Capitalism to the other ninety nine percent of the population? Capitalism relies on a consumer culture, in which the major part of the population, who do the labour to produce but now, cannot afford to buy the products they are producing. The meltdown; as 2008 drew to a close it was obvious that too many workers had been reduced to subsistence wages, or less, or were unemployed and could no longer afford to buy even unessential products or services, never mind paying their credit card debt and mortgages.

The real economy is based on national resources, the means of production, and labour. When labour is applied to converting a resource into a product, wealth is produced. During the mercantilist period there were many artisans, tradesmen, and farmers who produced and traded their products and services with no need for a capitalist middleman. When the industrial revolution began in Britain, the aristocrats who ruled the country provided the needed capital to finance railroads and factories, the aristocrats owned the land, instead of the government, and as a result the British aristocracy has survived to this day as capitalists. By stealing the commons, and natural resources from the people feudalism continued with a new label.

Europeans and North Americans fought against capitalism until after the Second World War when socialist democratic policies were adopted, workers were allowed to form unions and a reasonable degree of egalitarianism was instituted; this became known as Social Democracy. Capitalism and Socialism coexisted as Social Democracy for nearly three decades following the Second World War; life was good for working people, and then laissez-faire capitalism made a comeback called globalization and "free" trade. Jobs were eliminated by sending the work to developing and third world countries where labour was dirt cheap. Unions were attacked, wages were frozen or rolled back, and cuts to social programs began in order to increase profits for corporations.

Capitalism de-regulated, and the big change of face.

In the 1970s Margaret Thatcher and Ronald Reagan introduced neo-liberalism: the deregulation of capitalism; that eventually lead to the globalization of poverty96. Social democracy was ended. Canada and other Anglo countries followed Britain, wages were frozen for many workers, strikes were broken or prohibited, unions were busted and labour conditions seriously deteriorated to raise productivity we were told. As capitalists, and their corporations gained power government services were cut, and user fees introduced, social services were reduced, and funding for health care was slashed. Part time jobs began replacing full time jobs, reducing or eliminating social benefits; forcing many people to take on two or more jobs in order to survive. In Canada unemployment insurance benefits were cut, to increase productivity and more than five billion dollars in the unemployment insurance fund was expropriated by the government and used to reduce the national debt97. Productivity increased and profits for capitalists and corporations sky rocketed; all at the expense of working people. The rich got richer while the people were left to suffer and wonder what happened.

Since the 1980s it has become impossible for most working class couples to get married, and have children, without both of them working to support a family, unless one of them is a banker or had a job on Wall Street. This is a direct result of a combination of government policies that widened the inequality gap; lowered real wages for workers, imposed user fees for most public services, increased income tax rates on low income workers, and reduced income taxes on higher paid professionals, the wealthy, and corporations. These government policies have severely reduced most of the social gains made earlier in the 20th century that had created a prosperous working class in which a man could support a family, and his wife was able to stay at home with the children.

Further compounding the problem, when our government surrendered it's ability to control the economy and the wealth of the working people to the corporations; private and government pension funds that were formerly invested in the government, and used to reduce foreign borrowing to finance government debt by way of bonds etc were handed over for speculation to the private market and big losses occurred. As a result, working people have to make higher pension fund contributions while those who manipulated the funds skimmed off personal fortunes. The sheeple continue to be fleeced in every conceivable way possible. The bankers and fund managers who conducted the massive rip offs became wealthy98 and the bankers are still rewarding themselves for their failure with multi million dollars bonuses and perks thanks to government bail out money in the U.S.,99,100,101.

In Canada our mixed economy has become progressively more and more capitalistic; and like the game of monopoly, those with the least are reduced to nothing, and those with the most continue to get even more as the wealth of the country is concentrated in fewer and fewer hands with the majority of Canadians now totally dependent on their next pay cheque102.

We now have food banks and large numbers of homeless people, unheard of in the 50s and 60s, and this problem has been getting progressively worse year by year.

Family life is almost non existent for those at the bottom of the food chain, with both parents working, often long hours, in some cases holding down several part time jobs for low wages and no benefits. A Dec 10th 2008 headline read: According to UNICEF. "Canada ties for last among developed countries for child services"103. The neglect of the children due to the absence of a family life, and cuts to social programs, has created many problems including a growing juvenile crime rate. Children left of their own to grow up watching TV, playing computer games, or hanging out on the street have no sense of family life, and little empathy for others; as Einstein pointed out people growing up in a capitalist system, learn only capitalist values. When people are born and grow up in a country with a single ideology; a limited education, and a corporate news network they are very effectively brainwashed.

The "free" trade agreement with the US in 1987 was a very decisive turning point in Canada's history; the only way workers standard of living could go was down. Canada can not have free trade with another country without being on an equal footing to compete, and in order to have free trade with the U.S. our standard of living had to drop to match theirs. Free trade with the U.S. gave us massive unemployment, food banks, second hand clothing stores; and imported food produced in the US by migrant workers for sub standard wages.

Expanding free trade to NAFTA and including Mexico sent both Canada and the US toward a lower standard of living to compete with the Mexicans. If the capitalists continue to get their way we will all be competing with the third world's standard of living. Looking at other first world countries around the world it is easy to see that of all the first world countries the US is the least desirable place for working people to live; and Canada once the number 1 country in the world to live in has been narrowing the gap becoming more and more like the U.S..

The most significant features of the best countries to live in are the degree of equality in wages between those at the top and those at the bottom of the income scale, and their income tax rates. The best countries have the lowest inequality in wages and a progressive income tax system in which income tax rates are higher as income increases. These countries also have the lowest crime rates, as well as universal health care, and very good public education. It is also notable that these countries have more democratic governments as demonstrated by their voter turn out rates and referendums on important issues such as military spending and free trade: direct democracy104.

It is readily apparent why the US is rated the least desirable place to live, gross inequality in wages, unfair income taxes, the largest prison population in the world, no universal health care, and a poor public educational system. Understanding how this was allowed to happen in what is touted as the first representative democracy in modern times is very difficult with the multiple meanings for words that have come into use to obscure the truth; but to put it simply, it is deregulated capitalism; the loss of democracy to corporations.

The Face of Capitalism today in South America

Neo-liberalism, and capitalism are equally reviled by most of the population throughout South America as a result of governments imposing neo-liberal policies in the past; that have put their countries into debt and reduced the standard of living for the majority as has also happened in much of the western world105. What is different in south America is that more and more people have recently become educated and realise who their real enemy is, and they have begun to acquire public media. While only a few countries have elected socialist governments to date we can expect to see many more because the people have realised that it is useless to vote for traditional political parties, but by banding their various social groups together they can form a formidable political force that is capable of taking power106.

While most of the former military dictatorships have lost power in South America there are still several neo-liberal U.S. backed capitalist oligarchies clinging to power; controlling their media, and backed by US government money such as Columbia107. In June of 2009 a military coup was carried out in Honduras with US backing to evict a president who was attempting to present a referendum on the question of adopting a democratic constitution by the people, like Venezuela, and Bolivia had done.108. The coup was engineered to prevent the people from rewriting their constitution and making it democratic109. The coup was still receiving funding from the U.S. three months later despite claims to the contrary110,111. Condemned by most of the world Honduras was kicked out of the Organization of American States, and most countries withdrew their ambassadors.

The coup in Honduras was followed by a US plan to establish a number of additional military bases, and a navel installation in Columbia that is viewed by most countries in South America as paving the way for an assault on revolutionary Venezuela, and again using Honduras as it did in the 1980s as a launching pad for attacks on Central American countries112,113.

With the realisation by the people that imposed neo-liberal "democracies" are not in the peoples interests their days are numbered; mass protests continue despite the murders and violent repression. Education is a powerful tool that has only recently began to be available to many people in South America.

In Argentina, the National Popular Children's Movement, (MCP), for the past six years has been mobilizing organizations across the country in a "Hunger is a Crime Campaign114." This year marked the largest demonstration to date with well over 50,000 participants representing various provinces and diverse organizations throughout Argentina.115 With the growing success this year despite violent repression, leaders of the groups participating now realise their combined power is a strong political force. Argentineans have been leading the way in occupying and operating factories closed by the owners, and proving that they do not need bosses to run profitable businesses116.

Brazil was one of the first countries in the world to implement and experience the full effects of neo-liberalism and one of the first to reject it. In 1999 more than 100,000 people from all over Brazil marched in Brasilia in the biggest protest ever against President Cardoso's economic policies117. The protest was sponsored by the five main leftist opposition Parties; the PT, the Brazilian Socialist Party (PSB), the Democratic Workers Party (PDT), the Brazilian Communist Party (PCB) and the Communist Party of Brazil (PCdoB)--along with about 80 other organizations of "civil society," including the CUT, the Landless Rural Workers Movement (MST), and student groups118.

Lula, said the opposition was calling for a program "to construct an industrial policy, to carry out land reform, create financing for small and medium sized farmers, channel public resources to help small, and medium sized businesses, end illiteracy, stop the privatization of public universities and not let them privatize the Federal Savings Bank, the Bank of Brazil, Petrobras [the state oil company] and the post office."119 Since Lula was elected he has been slow in implementing these policies; he leans to the left, but is not a socialist, but some progress has been made. The marchers in Brasilia in 1999 also protested the acquittal of three police officers charged with the murder of 19 peasants who had been acquitted of murder; a decision that shocked millions, the massacre had been recorded by news crews on film clearly showing police agents firing repeatedly into the crowd at close range. In a separate demonstration, a group of farmers continued to camp out in the capital to pressure Congress to approve a package to write off at least $9.2 billion in debt to the IMF120.

Twenty years after the financial collapse and rejection of neo-liberal policies Brazil has become the country with the leading economy in South America121. China has replaced the U.S. as Brazils' number one trading partner sparing Brazil another collapse with the U.S. meltdown.122. When the meltdown started President Lulu was asked about it and replied: "Ask Bush, it's his crises not mine." Lulu also commented that the days were over when the US sneezed Brazil caught pneumonia."

In 1984, a group of nearly a hundred "landless" farmers from across Brazil met in to debate the founding of a movement for agrarian reform which would unite landless campesinos and farm workers from around the country. It was very a difficult campaign where even today less than two percent of landowners still control nearly half of the land total. However twenty five years later, the tiny Landless Worker's Movement (MST) has grown to a formidable force that has forced the expropriation of 35 million acres; and 370,000 families now live on their own land producing their own food. The MST movement has built hundreds of public schools and taught tens of thousands of its members how to read and write. MST members have formed 400 associations and cooperatives to collectively produce and share their own food. However today, at least 100,000 families are still living in encampments waiting for land.123

Former colonial governments instituted latifundia, the practice of giving huge land holdings to elites from the homeland, and or officers in their militaries for services rendered; and are still prevalent in most South American countries today. These latifundia originated under colonial law and allowed forced or slave labour. In post-colonial times, ending the dominance of the latifundia system by implementing agrarian reforms became a popular goal of several governments in the region. Land redistribution is still a major problem in many countries in South America. Huge parcels of land that were given away, or sold by colonial regimes; large tracts of land were just taken over from the native population with no legal justification. In some countries neo-liberalism has led to corporate takeovers of huge tracts of land; often by US companies, for monoculture. Monoculture is blamed for the shortage of food in several countries where growing soy beans for export to the U.S. and since the meltdown to China has become big business124.

Argentina has a huge problem with latifundia and soy production that has spread to neighbouring countries Uruguay, Brazil, Bolivia and Paraguay through neo-liberalism making the area the largest soy producing region in the world125. Corporations are responsible for most of the problems today monopolizing land needed for domestic food production, the destruction of the rain forests, and using the land to produce soy for export. Corporations buy out or rent land from the traditional small farmers, putting many people out of work, who then attack the rain forests for land to develop for agriculture in a never ending cycle126.

The three major agribusinesses in Paraguay are U.S. trans-national corporations: agri-business giants Archer Daniel Midland, Bunge and Cargill, and the genetically modified seeds guru Monsanto127. Despite having a democratically elected president who promised land reform the government of Paraguay is still controlled be neo-liberal interests, and the people are kept at heal by a US trained military128.

Capitalism in decline

The decline of neo-liberalism was evident long before nine eleven129,130. Despite misleading reports in the western media to the contrary, much of the world has remained primarily socialist, capitalism has merely been allowed to coexist with various restrictions in many western countries where market economies, fair trade and globalization have gained a foothold. The western countries that have permitted deregulation of capitalism are suffering the full effects of the meltdown and negative growth in their GNP, while Socialist, Communist, and Islamic countries have continued to experience growth and expansion.

The only adverse effects many socialist countries experienced were due to a lack of exports to western countries that could no longer afford them. The attacks in western countries, on wages, and social programs that began in the 1970s have reduced so many people to poverty, and they no longer have money to spend for anything that is not essential. The standard of living, for many people in western countries, not just in North America, has deteriorated so badly that discontent and revolution is fermenting again as it did in the 18th and 19th centuries. With 1% of the population in the U.S. controlling

90% of the wealth there not very many potential consumers left with money to revive the dying economy131.

The emerging BRIC economies Brazil, Russia, India, and China are not only predominately Socialist; their economies continue to grow while Western economies continue to shrink as capitalism collapses in North America, and Europe. In South America, countries that have reverted to Socialism such as Venezuela and Brazil who have re-nationalised their banks escaped most of the effects of the meltdown. While US trade is in freefall and the US is unable to advance its "free" trade on the rest of the world China, Brazil, and Russia have been busy concluding fair trade agreements around the world. As a result China is looking at an 8 to 9% increase in GDP this year while the US forecast is minus 2-3%.

Capitalism in Greece

Greece, the birthplace of democracy, was paralysed for more than two weeks before the Christmas break in 2008, by protests and strikes that spread to other European countries in a vast anti capitalist uprising. President Karamanlis and his right wing New Democrats are hanging onto office by a single seat in the 300-member Greek parliament. His Capitalist dominated government like the US had agreed to give €28 billion to the bankers, while cutting social services, pensions and forcing privatizations of public services. He has blamed the protests on "enemies of democracy" saying there will be no leniency for the rioters. While it would be correct if he had said "enemies of capitalism" to say enemies of democracy is an outright lie. After months of protests and demands for the government to resign Karamanlis called an election and lost big time to the socialists in 2009.

As Einstein pointed out, there is no democracy in a capitalist society. If there is one single thing the Greek people know for a certainty, it is that Greece has not been allowed to have a democracy for a very long time, thanks to the U.S..

Democracy in Greece was prohibited after WW2, when Truman and Churchill divided Europe up after the Second World War, and

Greece slid into civil war, fought between communists and nationalists. During the five-year war, the US supported the nationalists, because they were desperate to ensure that capitalism would prevail. As a result it took 25 years from the end of the civil war for communists and their supporters to be fully accepted back into Greek society; and resentment over their mistreatment continues today.

In the 1970s Greek retaliation began when a rocket was fired at the US embassy hitting the eagle emblem, and many Greeks reacted with great satisfaction to the dawn rocket attack in Athens. On November 17th 1975 Richard Welch, the CIA station chief, was killed outside his home in Athens, and the killing of three US diplomats followed in retaliation for American support of the right-wing military dictatorship that ruled Greece with an iron fist from 1967 to 1974. The colonels' regime began to falter after a student uprising in 1973, centred at the Athens Polytechnic, and on November 17 that year the colonels sent in tanks to crush the revolt.

The younger Greek generation's disdain of the US has been fuelled not just by stories told by parents and grandparents, but also by US foreign policy, most recently by Bush's invasions of Iraq and Afghanistan, and the US backed genocide in Gaza by Israel. The heavily fortified US embassy is a focal point for dissent in Athens, and the wars in Iraq and Afghanistan, are widely opposed in Greece, and regarded as despicable acts of US Imperialism. The Israeli attack on Gaza at the end of 2008 created massive protests in Greece, and the blame was placed equally on the US and Israel for the massacre. Amnesty International has called on Greek authorities to end the "unlawful and disproportionate use of force by police" and noted "mounting evidence of police beatings and ill-treatment of peaceful demonstrators." Police beatings, murder, and ill treatment of peaceful demonstrators have become standard practice in many capitalist dominated countries as we witnessed in North America beginning with the Battle of Seattle, and Quebec City protests. Support for Palestine was widespread in Europe with mass demonstrations against Israel, and the US in many countries.

Capitalism in Latin America

Cubans recently celebrated the 50th anniversary of their revolution against capitalism, and have been experiencing good economic growth and record tourism. Venezuela has been undergoing a peaceful revolution for ten years now in pursuit of a 21st century form of socialism and Bolivia is following Venezuela in nationalizing key industries, educating the people and providing health care; and these countries experienced little or no effects of the capitalist meltdown.

The move toward socialism in Latin America has been led by grass roots organizations putting aside their differences and banding together to support a new political party or leader for the common good. Latin American countries that are in various stages in setting up a common market and financial system include, Argentina, Brazil, Bolivia, Ecuador, Uruguay, Cuba, and Venezuela. Venezuela has been leading the way bringing China and Russia into Latin American trade, joint ventures, and banking. These joint ventures among socialist countries do not hand over natural resources to international companies, ownership of the resources remains with the people. Thanks to trade with Russia and China many exports that stopped going to the US during the meltdown readily found new markets. Neo-liberalism is extremely unpopular throughout Latin America, as is capitalism in general.

Neo-liberalism was ended in Bolivia with a bold new constitution that empowers the country's ethnic communities with access to education and healthcare much like that of Venezuela. After Bolivia's new constitution was approved in a national referendum President Evo Morales, an indigenous, former union organiser, addressed the people saying:

"Here begins a new Bolivia. Here we begin to reach true equality."

Indigenous people had formerly been prohibited from even entering that same plaza. Bolivia is South America's poorest country, with 62% of the population self-identifying as indigenous, and about the same percentage living under the poverty line. Many who support

Morales and his Movement Toward 21st Century Socialism (MAS) party see the new constitution as granting long-overdue rights to the indigenous majority. Morales speech continued...

> "I want you to know something, the colonial state ends here. Internal colonialism and external colonialism ends here. Sisters and brothers, neo-liberalism ends here too."

Among many other changes, the new constitution empowers Bolivia's indigenous and Afro-Bolivian communities, establishes broader access to basic services, education and healthcare, limits the size of large land purchases, expands the role of the state in the management of natural resources and the economy and prohibits the existence US military bases on Bolivian soil.

Having rejected neo-liberalism, three countries in Latin America are now in the process of bringing about real democratic reforms, and improving the human progress of their people. Bolivia became the third Latin American country to make human progress possible through education and health care a reality.

Capitalism in Iceland

Iceland was an early victim of the meltdown, because the country had become a financial banking centre and the banks were loaded with worthless U.S. derivatives. The country simply did not have enough reserve funds to cover the worthless debt and had to resort to a loan from the IMF.

This is a classic case of imperialism; a country is plunged into debt by capitalists and when it can find no other recourse it is forced to submit to the IMF, putting the people in bondage to pay the debt. The people were told that there would be cuts to social programs, reductions in wages, higher taxes, and privatization of public property. Immediately the people began protesting and demanding the resignation of the government. Icelanders are primarily Nordic in origin the country was originally settled by anarchist Danes who instituted the first anarchist system of government. After months of demonstrations and protests the government was forced to resign in January 2009 and call an election.

The banks should have been permitted to go bankrupt, but capitalist governments make a practice of bailing them out at the expense of the public. Private for profit banks should not be the responsibility of the public and like any other failed business they should go bankrupt. If neo-liberalism was ethical the US government would have stood behind the debt that the U.S. private banks were responsible for in other countries, but of course that did not happen; they just gave the bankers more money. At any rate it will be interesting to see what kind of government will be elected in Iceland and if the people will permit a new government to pay the bankers debts.

Capitalism in Hong Kong

Hong Kong although it has been returned to China still operates much as it did under British rule however Chinese ethics have made a big difference.

Hong Kong's regulator, the Securities and Futures Commission, reprimanded a Hong Kong brokerage for failing to properly train its' sales staff and conduct proper research into Lehman products and ordered Sun Hung Kai, one of Hong Kong's largest non-bank financial institutions to repay investors for their loses. Some 310 investors will recover around 11 million dollars lost in worthless US derivatives pedalled by Lehman brothers.132 A Sun Hung Kai advertisement had described the Lehman-backed mini-bonds as a product "letting you invest with peace of mind", even though the small print did mention that there was "a high degree of risk". This sends a message not only to brokerage dealers but also to other governments that permitting the dealing of questionable securities is unethical, and it the responsibility of governments to protect the public.

The face of capitalism has changed radically in many western countries since the 1970s and the changes have resulted in gross inequality such as exists in the US today where the wealth of the three wealthiest individuals is greater than one hundred million of their fellow citizens, and one percent of the population hold ninety percent of all the wealth. If this continues the people in the US and other countries where de-regulated Capitalism is allowed to go unrestrained will discover that they are no better off, or freer than their ancestors were during the age of feudalism.133

The level of inequality in some US cities now rivals that of Africa according to a recent UN study.134 Since capitalism in the US, and Britain, were freed from many restraints during the 1970s and 80s, inequality has been growing at an accelerated pace, concentrating wealth in fewer and fewer hands. Neo-liberalism, promoted as free trade, and globalization, is regarded throughout most of the world as Imperialism. As Capitalist Oligarchs and Corporations have gained strength, more and more people throughout the world have been denied, their basic rights to education, health care, housing, and even drinking water.

In the US where the big three in Detroit were once heralded around the world as the glowing example of what was possible under capitalism today is proof of the failure of capitalism. The once powerful unions that created a great standard of living for the auto workers have been turned into assistants of the governments bailing out the capitalists, and exporting their members jobs to developing countries. After receiving billions in bail outs from the US and Canadian governments GM expects to soon be importing many vehicles from China in the coming year in addition to those being assembled in Mexico thanks to taxpayers money and auto workers pension funds. Call it what you want; neo-liberalism, "free" trade, globalization, or imperialism; it is Capitalism running amok.

Imperialism is accomplished by either of two means; capitalism, acquiring the natural resources and means of production through the manipulation of money, or war. Capitalism is facing growing resistance; the end of any possible world "free" trade agreement, new regional currencies, similar to the Euro, and the new 21st century socialism. The U.S. dollar is no longer trusted or wanted in much of the world. War now appears to be inevitable unless the people can gain control of the government. During the last decade, both wars and unrestrained capitalism have been running wild in the world as capitalists attempted to impose their culture around the world.

The World Bank and the International Monetary Fund, controlled primarily by U.S. capitalists, have been very instrumental in establishing imperialism in many third world and developing countries. Many South American countries have thrown off the yoke of the IMF and in addition nationalized natural their resources and begun giving the land back to the people. It is very hard for capitalists to accept that they do not have the right to own the natural resources of the planet.

De-regulated capitalism has resulted in two economies, the real economy, and a cyber economy. The cyber economy allows corporations and very wealthy individuals to manipulate things that they don't even own such as stocks, currencies, and the price of commodities such as oil, and move their money from one country to another electronically.

Looking back over the past few months at the end of December 2008 we saw the price of oil drop from $147, a barrel to $36. In a market economy it would be logical to assume that the market had been saturated and there was no longer a demand for oil production but that was not the case. Oil was still priced far above the cost of production for most of the oil that was being produced in the world, so how did it suddenly come down so far in price, why didn't it go lower, and why did it climb so high to begin with? Cyber capitalism the other economy is where speculators make money, when the price goes up by buying futures, and again when prices drop, by short selling stocks and currencies that they do not even own. There is no question that some of the international oil companies reaped record profits but even greater profits were taken by the cyber economy manipulators.

The Global Meltdown in 2008 totally discredited the Capitalistic system because of its Cyber economy, and Ponzi schemes. The meltdown revealed that the US economy survived the last decades based on massive fraud that created the US housing bubble and then flooded the world with worthless derivatives, like the mother of all Ponzi schemes135,136. The US government is on the verge of bankruptcy with the largest debt in the history of the world, and attempting to borrow even more money from wealthy nations to continue its' attempt to dominate and control the world. On their way to a two trillion dollar deficit in mid 2009 the US was still expanding the size of its' military and the number of new bases around the world.

When the people of any country are reduced to subsistence wages or less, discontent is bound to follow. US unemployment was officially at 9.8 % in the fall of 2009 and growing; the real unemployment is unknown since only people eligible for unemployment insurance are counted. You do not need to be an economist to know that an economy can not work when the people have no money to spend. With massive unemployment, hunger, and homelessness due to the lack of money in circulation among the general population discontent can lead to anarchy, rebellion, and revolution. The repression of dissent has been US policy for quite some time that is why the US has the largest prison population in the world. Aided by the corporate media who do not report most demonstrations or actions against the system, most of the people remain ignorant of what is going on in their own country.

Since the 1970s when Reagan took the US dollar off of the gold standard Islamic banking has been growing by 15% per year and is now a trillion dollar business. Islamic bankers describe depositors as akin to partners, their money is invested, and they share in the profits or, theoretically, the losses that result. Rather than lend money to a home buyer and collect interest on it, an Islamic bank buys the property and then leases it to the buyer for the duration of the loan. The client pays a set amount each month to the bank, at the end of his contract he obtains full ownership. The payments are structured to include the cost of the house, plus a predetermined profit margin for the bank. Many western people have been attracted to this way of buying a house or an apartment, and the peace of mind that goes with it not having to worry about short term mortgages, and changing interest rates.

Islamic finance first aroused interest in the United States in the late 1990s. The Dow Jones Islamic Index was established in 1999, and the Dow Jones Islamic Fund, which invests in Shariah compliant companies, the following year. In 2004, the German state of Saxony-

Anhalt issued a 100 million-euro sovereign Islamic bond. That same year, the first Islamic bank opened in Britain, which now has six Islamic financial institutions, including a retail bank. While the largest Islamic banks are located in the Persian Gulf, Dubai Islamic Bank, Kuwait Finance House and Saudi Arabia's al-Rajhi Bank; Malaysia and London are also growing as major centres of Islamic banking.

Islamic banks have not suffered during the meltdown from investments in derivatives and speculation in futures and short selling because such practices are prohibited. No Islamic banks have gone broke, and no depositors have lost their money. What a different world we would be looking at today if all banking in the world had been Islamic.

The Final Stage of Capitalism

Karl Marx envisioned the final stage of Capitalism as being very close to where the US is at today; competition between Capitalists is now international and workers have had their wages so reduced in real terms that they no longer have any money to spend on products that they can not afford that economies are crumbling. With the Nations wealth concentrated in the hands of a few Capitalists the economy dies; with no customers continued production is unnecessary, and the workers lose their jobs compounding the problem. With millions of families homeless and record levels of unemployment people become desperate, and hungry. At this stage revolution is a very real danger and the country would then probably go to war in order to destroy surplus production, and reduce the population.

In 1844 Marx did not foresee the possibility of a large scale terrorist attack being used to control the population but that is also a very real possibility in the US today. The situation is quite similar in Britain where social programs have been severely cut and unemployment is also soaring.

Will the US become social-able or continue with its' Wars, have another Terrorist Attack, or a Revolution? The election of Obama created high expectations for reform and change. More than a million false front pages of The New York Times were circulated in New York and Los Angeles on November 12, 2008 dated 4 July 2009 announcing a complete withdrawal from Iraq, and the implementation of numerous socialist programs for the people. The sheer size of this operation to print and deliver more than a million free copies on both coasts of the US demonstrates the support for radical change. Could Obama deliver if he wanted to? However by July 4th 2009 Obama had not only failed to deliver on any of his election promises he had had been credited with his first coup in Honduras and ordered more troops to go to Afghanistan. In August it was announced that the US was setting up five more military bases in Columbia; at this rate Obama is proceeding with war plans even faster than Bush.

The G 29 meeting 5 November 2008 failed to produce any reform only a commitment to study the problem. Many countries left the meeting very dissatisfied, and began implementing their own changes for a new financial order. The president of China went to South America, and Cuba, to sign trade agreements with several countries that China did more than a hundred billion dollars in trade with the year before. The EU also left determined to proceed with unilateral changes, and was opening talks with Russia on joint trade and monetary policies, that could lead to further expansion of the EU. Many Latin American countries led by Venezuela, are relatively unaffected by the meltdown because they have escaped the clutches of the IMF, begun developing their natural resources for the benefit of their people, and started their own development bank and regional trading block that does not use dollars. This Bolivarian bank is funded primarily by Venezuelan oil, but Russia, and China are also investors. As new blocks form with regional currencies like the EU, China, and Latin America, the power of the US dollar is shrinking in the world.

Greed and fear rule US Capitalism; coupled with unethical business practices, and Oligarchs manipulating the value of stocks and currencies. In Oct. 2008 much of the world was in the worst financial crises in history. Laissez faire Capitalism: US and Anglo Imperialism has lowered the standards of living for the majority of the population in every country that has adopted it; and was under attack before nine eleven diverted the world's attention. The World Bank and the International Monetary Fund controlled and directed by the USA and have served as major tools for Imperialism. In November 2008, Britain went cap in hand to Socialist China to bank role the IMF and World Bank; it was a bit much to expect, and China declined. Since then after demanded changes were made within the IMF China, and Russia have contributed to the fund.

China is a Socialist country that has been supporting third world countries with loans and grants with no strings attached, unlike the IMF and WB; and as a result has greatly expanded its sphere of influence and gained access to much needed imports of energy and natural resources while helping third world countries further their own social agendas and stay free of the IMF. While China as the largest single creditor to the USA has a vested interest in keeping the USA from bankruptcy it is ridiculous to expect them to help perpetuate Western Imperialism which is in direct opposition to Socialist principles. Since most countries except the USA and Britain have strong Socialist political parties that often form the government and, provide a higher standard of living for their people it is difficult to imagine that neo-liberal capitalism now proven to be dysfunctional can prevent the changes that are being demanded. China was also asked to supply troops for the war in Afghanistan, another no brainer. China has many UN peacekeeping commitments, but their government and people are opposed to wars of aggression. In addition, the wars in Iraq is not a UN operation; it is a U.S. war with unwilling NATO support.

The war in Afghanistan is a US adventure in imperialism that NATO countries were reluctantly sucked into; and few have really embraced. Many people, and countries do not believe that nine eleven could have taken place without inside cooperation by the government; that it was simply a means of suppressing opposition to Capitalism, and US, British, imperialism. Iraq was on the verge of switching from dollars to Euros for oil when it was attacked. In the US there is a large organization of war veterans for peace that is recognised by the UN as a (NGO), non-governmental organization, that has been protesting the invasion of Iraq since it began. Veterans of the war in Iraq have been calling for the arrest and prosecution of Bush and Cheney for conducting an illegal war, and war crimes. There is a great deal of dissatisfaction, and unrest in the US with wars, that are bankrupting the country, and the financial meltdown that is leaving many families homeless and unemployed.

The US has been making incursions into Pakistan that are causing serious repercussions and recently conducted a strike in Syria. The big question now is whether the USA will launch an attack on another country and possibly start WW3, have another terrorist attack, a bloody revolution, or change its policies and adapt to the realities. The US is on the verge of bankruptcy and other countries are not willing to loan more money to the U.S. unless there are major changes to the financial system, a big reduction in deficit spending, and withdrawal from Iraq and Afghanistan. There are rumours that the US will attempt to suck Canada and Mexico into a common currency called the Amero in an attempt to prop up their unwanted dollar in the rest of the world.

The Global credit crunch has once again highlighted the fragility and abuses of Capitalism, as the fallout from the credit crunch and the wider economic crisis continues, demands for alternatives are growing. EU and Asian leaders are demanding sweeping changes, the Gulf countries are speeding up efforts to have a single currency, Islamic banking is expanding around the world. China and Russia the world's two fastest growing economies are abandoning the use of the dollar in their mutual trade. Germans want to nationalise their banks and key industries. Britain "Cap in Hand" asked China and the Gulf States to bail out the world's financial system.

When the fallout settles we can expect to see a number of regional currencies; the US dollar will no longer be in circulation in many parts of the world, and vastly different rules will govern global Cyber Capitalism in various regions where it may continue to exist in a greatly reduced role.

In October 2009 The Bank of the South went into operation in South America and has a common currency for member countries similar to the Euro in Europe. China has begun to use it's currency in dealings with Asian trading partners as it debuts as a world currency. China is letting the dollar sink slowly to protect it's investment in the U.S. but the dollar has been sliding steadily as China went on a shopping spree around the world to get rid of as much of its' U.S. foreign exchange as possible.

Islamic banking has been growing rapidly in the Middle East and spreading into Europe and South East Asia. Russia and China have eliminated dollars in their trade with each other. Iran no longer accepts dollars for its' oil, and on it goes as much of the world finds a safer currency to do business with. Both Lenin and Karl Marx as well as other philosophers predicted the bubbles, and crashes, that were inevitable in Capitalism, and also an end of Capitalism when the wealth became concentrated into the hands of a few Oligarchs, and working people were reduced to subsistence wages in the Capitalists quest for greater profits; when the people no longer had money to spend the economy would collapse.

Since 1955 progressive income taxes in the U.S. for the wealthiest have dropped from 91%, and after loopholes 51.2 % to 17.2 % in 2006. Corporate taxes dropped from 33% in 1955 to 7.4% in 2003. Wages for most workers in the U.S. did not increase from 1979 to 1998 and the median wage was below the 1979 level, despite an increase in productivity of 44.5%. From 2002 to 2004 median household income dropped by $1,669.00137.

Since "free" trade began CEO's salaries in the U.S. have risen from 30 to 40 times that of a worker to 317 to 525 times that of a worker. Corporations no longer make better products to make money they take over other companies and lay off workers. Downsizing is how they make money now and collect multi million dollar bonuses138. This scenario has much in common with what has happened in Canada, and Britain.

However the decline of U.S. influence and steadily falling dollar have severely crippled plans for a world takeover by the capitalists with their printing presses producing money now that few countries are willing to accept U.S. dollars. As October 2009 progressed the U.S. dollar had been in steady decline against most world currencies for weeks. In South America the Bank of the South had commenced operation. Iran is being threatened with attack as Iraq was just before it was invaded because it would no longer sell oil for dollars. China is increasing the range of its' use of the RMB in place of dollars, and the Euro and Japanese yen are currently the favoured currencies for a safe haven for westerners. Obama was reconsidering the U.S. occupation of Afghanistan despite his military generals' demands for forty thousand more troops.

Capitalism needs wars to survive, the workers in the population must be kept occupied and divided against each other whether in a regular work force or not; wars help keep people occupied, and divided. The war on terror like the war on drugs is a make work project to keep the sheeple occupied, and make the wealthy, wealthier. With unemployment in the U.S. officially approaching ten percent, and realistically closer to twenty percent; unrest is rising.

The war on drugs, like the prohibition of alcohol in the roaring twenties has simply created vast opportunities for illegal profiteering; unsafe streets, a greatly increased rate of crime, more police at public expense and larger prison populations. The war on drugs is war without end, like the war on terror. These wars help to keep the population divided against each other and divert attention from the manipulators who are stealing their lives and their futures.

Globalization

As David Rockefeller admitted in his memoirs there is no question that a conspiracy has been going on in the world for quite some time to create a global political and economic government, and that it is working against the best interests of the people of the US.

"For more than a century, ideological extremists at either end of the political spectrum have seized upon well-publicized incidents to attack the Rockefeller family for the inordinate influence they claim we wield over American political and economic institutions. Some even believe we are part of a secret cabal working against the best interests of the United States, characterizing my family and me as 'internationalists' and of conspiring with others around the world to build a more integrated global political and economic structure - one world, if you will. If that's the charge, I stand guilty, and I am proud of it."

– David Rockefeller, Memoirs, 6-11-6

Chapter Six

The changing face of Socialism

Socialism according to the Encyclopaedia Britannica

"A Social, and economic doctrine, that calls for public rather than private ownership or control of property and natural resources. According to the socialist view, individuals do not live or work in isolation but live in cooperation with one another. Furthermore, everything that people produce is in some sense a social product, and everyone who contributes to the production of a good, is entitled to a share in it. Society as a whole, therefore, should own or at least control property for the benefit of all its members."

Socialism like capitalism varies from one country to another.

Socialists believe that the only real wealth in the world is derived from labour and natural resources; and that the natural resources in a country belong to the people; not an individual, a state, province, or corporation. Socialists also acknowledge that some people work much harder than others for wages and should be paid accordingly within reasonable limits. Socialists believe that pubic utilities and services belong to the public, and should not be privatised for profit. Many Socialists also believe that that production of goods, and products, should be regulated by government standards, and inspection, for quality, and safety; and that goods and products that simply waste raw materials to produce profit, at the expense of the environment should be banned.

The primary objective of Socialists is to achieve a relatively egalitarian society, in a market economy, where no one lives in poverty and misery, while others live in absolute luxury; a society where the streets are safe and no one has to live in fear of a home invasion; and the environment is respected. Universal health care, and education are viewed as basic rights by socialists; democracy can only function with a healthy, and informed educated population.

Socialism in China

Contrary to Capitalist media in North America China is not a Capitalist country, China is a socialist country in the process of developing a market economy with Chinese characteristics, as Hugo Chavez is attempting to create what he calls 21st century Socialism in Venezuela. Socialism in its most basic form requires public not private ownership of national banks and natural resources. By opening up to a market economy China has lifted a large part of its' population out of poverty and been enabled to install many social programs for the benefit of its' most disadvantaged people. China has also made huge contributions to third world countries with health care; Chinese medical-assistance teams have conducted more than 260 million treatments in 69 foreign countries and regions since 1963. In Dec 08 the minister of Health Chen Zhu said: "… the Chinese government is going to strengthen cooperation in medicine and health with developing countries for the health of mankind and social progress."

In dealing with the global meltdown China had no need to bail out its' National Banks and acknowledging that the domestic market economy was of great importance, is developing new financial institutions that are intended to offer better financial support for smaller enterprises, to avoid the widespread bankruptcies and massive lay-offs characteristic of large monopolistic capitalist businesses.

The Chinese government is a dictatorship of the people, for the people, and by the people; in contrast the US government which is a dictatorship by Capitalist Corporations, for themselves and their wealthy friends. The US has done nothing comparable to promote human development, or health, in third world countries, or emerging economies like China, Cuba, and Venezuela; and does not even provide health care for its' own population. While Western Capitalist countries will continue to deteriorate during the meltdown pursuing neo-liberal policies: cutting social programs, reducing wages, and limiting access to education China is increasing social programs, creating universal health care, access to education, raising wages, and launching major infrastructure projects to create jobs.

It is important to note that despite having a population of 1.3 billion people, China has an unarmed police force, and perhaps the safest streets in the world. Can you imagine living in the U.S. or Canada with an unarmed police force?.

Going Socialist in Latin America

The era of armed revolutions is coming to an end in Latin America, and so have a number of neo-liberal "democracies". Successful recent revolutions have come about through the people rejecting traditional neo-liberal "democratic" parties in elections, and unifying all social organizations in support of a single new socialist party. Violence to instil or maintain governments is now the tool of neo-liberals and capitalist oligarchies.

Mass demonstrations despite brutal repression have brought down governments and forced change. Education, and an emerging public media are playing a large role in exposing neo-liberalism and capitalism for their role in creating the poverty and misery that has been plaguing their countries.

Until ten years ago when socialism began to take over there was not one country in South or Central America with an educated population, little health care, and almost no public media. The battle continues in all of these countries between the capitalist Oligarchs who still control most of the wealth and almost all of the media, but things are changing. Hugo Chavez in Venezuela, Evo Morales in Bolivia, Correa in Ecuador and most recently former Sandinista chief, Ortega in Nicaragua have eliminated illiteracy implementing socialist policies and programs beginning with universal health care.

The era of coups has not ended however. In 2002 a coup was carried out against Hugo Chavez of Venezuela but it was short lived when the population rose in protest despite a media blackout. In June 2009 a coup was carried out against Mel Zelaya the president of Honduras and despite mass protests, general strikes, and road blockades the perpetrators were still clinging to power more than three months later killing and disappearing people, brutally attacking the unarmed protesters, suspending all constitutional rights to protest, and shutting down all resistance media.

As 2008 came to an end Paraguay appears that it may be the next to go socialist; over a hundred social organizations banded together and staged a mass protest for three days, despite brutal police repression, that resulted in the president promising socialist land reforms. In September 2009 the new president of Paraguay refused to conduct military exercises with the U.S. in solidarity with Unasur and Mercosur139.

Socialism in Venezuela

In 1998 Hugo Chavez was elected President on the promise of leading the country into 21st Century Socialism. Ten years later Chavez had made very impressive gains for the countries workers and poor, against fierce opposition from the Oligarchs who owned most of the country; in a referendum he obtained the right to run for re-election. After nationalising the oil industry during his first mandate Chavez was able to finance many social programs, and begin new programs so that the people could begin to produce many products that were being imported and begin to grow their own food.

Venezuela now has the most democratic government in all of North, Central, and South America. Over two hundred delegates from 12 European countries met at a conference in London on Saturday 10 November 2008 in support of democracy and social progress in Venezuela140. In Britain more than fifty Members of the British Parliament commended Venezuelan democracy and signed a motion noting that the 2nd December referendum in Venezuela revealed the vibrancy of the democratic process in Venezuela.

Despite false accusations that Chavez was leading Venezuela down a path to dictatorship, this was the 12th national vote in Venezuela since 1998 when Hugo Chávez was first elected. The motion noted, the commitment to democracy is in direct contrast to the way that opponents of the Chávez government, have sought to overthrow it, through non-democratic means, including a US backed military coup in 2002. The British MPs, also offered ongoing support to the Chávez government's policies of advancing social equality; stating that they are confident that Hugo Chávez will continue to lead the fight against neo-liberalism in Latin America, supported by all those who wish to end the exploitation, of the people, and environment.

The strong support from British MPs is an important rebuttal to the constant misrepresentation in the mainstream US media, about the democratic record of the Chávez government141,142. Venezuela is one of the few countries in the world where both the constitution, and any revisions to it, must be approved by a majority of citizens in a national referendum.

Extreme poverty has been halved, illiteracy nearly eliminated, participation in education has more than doubled and free basic health care extended to nearly 20 million people, who had no access before. Unemployment has fallen to an historic low. The people of Venezuela have all been educated for the first time in their history, and were the first country in South America to achieve that distinction. In August 2008 the Chávez administration ordered one million laptop computers, especially designed for children as part of a $3 billion, bilateral trade agreement with Portugal. The computers feature digital cameras, a broadband internet connection, and will run on a version of Linux, consistent with Venezuela's gradual move away from Microsoft.

In October 2008 China launched Venezuela's first communications satellite, which will be used to broadcast tele-education, medical service, and public broadcasting covering most regions of South America and the Caribbean. The satellite is expected to have a fifteen year lifespan, and be of great importance to improve the living standards of people living in remote areas. This satellite is now shared with other Latin American countries in accordance with the goals of ALBA.

ALBA began as a social alliance between Cuba, and Venezuela that expanded to include Bolivia, Nicaragua, and Ecuador, and by August 2009 it had nine member counties in Latin America. ALBA's objectives are based on principles of cooperation, solidarity, and mutual assistance; the goal is to create a new Bolivarian Republic, independent of outside interests. Countries that join ALBA automatically receive assistance in eradicating illiteracy, education, and health care. "ALBA has denounced capitalism and proposed radical measures to place the burden of capitalisms current economic crises on the elites who created it, not workers and the poor 143."

The government of president Hugo Chavez created a new public health system and with an initiative called Barrio Adentro, that provides universal free health care. Through a cooperative agreement with Cuba, Chavez was able to bring thousands of Cuban primary care doctors and health care workers to underserved Venezuelan neighbourhoods, and Cuba has been training Venezuelans to take over. Venezuelan clinics experienced a six-fold increase in clinic visits in the first six months, and teams have been sent out to remote areas; some of which can only be accessed by boat.

Following the Cuban model Venezuela will begin training Haitians in 2009 as medical professionals through the Integral Community Medicine Program and the National Program for Training Educators, as part of a tri-lateral agreement between Venezuela, Cuba, and Haiti. Venezuela will send a contingent of teachers to Haiti to begin the training of new doctors and teachers. In March 2009, a process of selecting 50 Haitians to benefit from scholarships in Venezuela, will also begin.

By nationalizing the oil industry, Hugo Chavez enabled Venezuela to do something for the working people for the first time in their history. Since then other Corporations have been nationalised, including a National Bank and most recently a steel plant that was refusing to negotiate with striking workers. Private banks still operate and Chavez has promised to nationalise any that fail as a result of the global meltdown.

On December 11, 2008 Venezuela's Agriculture and Land Minister, Elias Jaua, announced that production of food crops in Venezuela has increased 52 percent in the last decade, and food is no longer in short supply; Venezuela now produces more than seventy percent of it's requirements144. The increase in food production has been dramatic; in three years beef production increased by 2 million head that fills 70% of the demand. During the past ten years meat consumption has increased from 280,000 tons to 540,000 tons annually. Similarly milk production has increased from 3 million litres a day to 6 million in the last three years, while the demand is estimated at 10 million litres per day145. Since 2001 the government has redistributed 5 million acres of idle or underused land to small farmers and state owned enterprises for food production. The land reform act was passed in 2001, but the elites who own or control most of the land are still terrorising and killing small farmers. As a result farmers' militias may be formed before the end of 2009 for self protection; these farmers' militias are to be coordinated by the National Bolivarian Militia and directed by the Bolivian Armed Forces146.

The current US meltdown is expected to have little effect on Venezuela because the country is now free from the shackles of the IMF, and World Bank, has very few of its' reserves in US dollars, and its banks did not get stuck with worthless US securities; however if oil prices remain at unusually low prices some restraints may have to be made on expenditures, such as subsidising heating oil prices for poor people in the US. The loss of export market in the U.S. was quickly replaced by increased exports to Brazil, Russia, China, and Japan147. While the US and Britain are bailing out their banks Venezuela is busy opening a thousand new banks for the common people, something else the people never had; to encourage the creation of small business in the domestic economy, and further self sufficiency in agriculture with a budget of 1.6 billion U.S. dollars for 2009,148. After the US refused to sell needed equipment to Venezuela the country turned to Brazil, China, Russia, and Japan for trade, and as a result is no longer dependent of the US for anything.

Socialism in Bolivia

Evo Morales was elected president of Bolivia in January 2006 on a promise of leading the country toward socialism, similar to what Hugo Chavez had done in Venezuela. Morales promised to nationalize the countries gas reserves and use the money to improve the lives of the people, and to create a constitutional assembly to create a new constitution. In January 2009 the new constitution was passed149.

Morales election followed years of protests by social organisations that included trade unions, indigenous, women's and youth groups who had no political party to represent them. The neo-liberal regime had been busy privatizing government companies, and services and withdrawing the government from the economy. Sound familiar? The countries mines, the main source of employment were gradually closed or privatized creating mass unemployment. Sixty-eight people had been killed and over 400 wounded, demanding the resignation of the government and nationalization of the gas, in the repression that followed.

The looting of Bolivia by neo-liberals reached its peak in 2000 when the World Bank demanded and facilitated the privatization of the water supply in the city of Cochambamba to a foreign multinational consortium led by London-based International Water Limited. In exchange Bolivia would receive $600 million in debt relief. Bechtel immediately raised water rates by 35 per cent, and in the drive for profit maximization a law was even briefly passed prohibiting people from collecting rainwater; for the majority of Bolivians this was the last straw. Democracy returned to Bolivia with a real democratic election won by Evo Morales in 2005. Water is again a basic right, not a commodity.

The Bolivian gas reserves were nationalized on May 1st 2006. In 2005 under the former regime the country had received $250 million for gas, by 2008 it was receiving $2.3 billion. The additional $2 billion plus has gone a long way toward improving the peoples lives; a small universal pension plan for men and women over the age of sixty, primary school grants to encourage children to finish school, and a nationwide literacy campaign with support from Cuba, and

Venezuela that made Bolivia the second South American country to become 100% free of illiteracy. Since 2005 Bolivia's foreign reserves have risen from 1,7 to 8.5 billion and in 2009 has the highest gdp in Latin America.

A constitutional assembly was formed in 2006 and in January 2009 the people of Bolivia in the movement toward socialism voted and passed the new constitution with nearly 62% of the population supporting it. The new constitution grants unprecedented rights to Bolivia's indigenous majority, and establishes broader access to basic services of education, and health care; it also expands the role of the government in the management of natural resources and the economy. Natural resources are now the property of the people and no future government will be able to hand them over to trans-national companies with out holding a national referendum150. With the passing of the new constitution President Evo Morales declared:

"I want you to know the colonial state ends here, Internal colonialism and external colonialism ends here. Sisters and brothers, neo-liberalism ends here too."

Bolivia was declared the third illiteracy free Latin American nation, after Cuba, and Venezuela, and President Evo Morales said, the eradication of this social ill constitutes a triumph over colonialism, and imperialism, which rejected social commitments. Bolivia's attainment of this status, follows Cuba in 1961, and Venezuela in 2005. The president described the achievement as one of commitment to continue driving forward on education and other social projects. In his speech, Morales, the leader of the Movement toward Socialism thanked Cuba and Venezuela for their help with the educational campaign. According to the president, it should be emphasized that 820,000 people had learned how to read and write and that almost 30,000 of those received instruction in their indigenous languages, Quechua and Aymara151.

Socialism in Ecuador

Ecuadorians approved a new constitution in September 2008 that provides expanded access to health care, social security, education, and increases government control over the economy. As in the new Bolivian constitution there are expanded indigenous rights as well as social welfare policies. President Correa had a high approval rating before the referendum because he had seized property from the elites who were responsible for the 1999 banking crises, increasing public funding, and terminating the US lease on a military base. Popular mobilizations had thrown out three presidents since 1997 who had followed the neo-liberal agenda of the US. In December 2008 Correa declared that Ecuador would not be making payments on the countries debt to the IMF saying the debt was illegal. Ecuadorians brought in their new constitution in September of 2008 with great expectations152.

The countries Indigenous peoples' movement has long claimed "the so called debt really belongs to the oligarchy." Because the people did not benefit from any part of it, they therefore owe nothing". Meanwhile Correa pledged to prioritise the "social debt" over debt to foreign creditors. Ecuadorians approved a new constitution in September 2008, and re-elected Rafael Correa in 2009. After his re-election the U.S. military was expelled from Ecuador, following the practice of other left leaning South American countries.

As in other South American countries that are undergoing peaceful revolution toward socialism Correa still faces very strong opposition from the elites and their friends in the US. Many of Correa's supporters are also not happy with his continued support for large scale mining companies and he could face an indigenous uprising if he does not act to curb the excesses of mining companies. Canadian mining company Corriente Resources is developing an open pit copper mine in Ecuador's southern Amazon region. The people are very concerned about protecting their water supply as well as being evicted from their own land153.

Socialism in Nicaragua

In January 2007 Daniel Ortega was re-elected president of Nicaragua after spending seventeen years in opposition. Ortega was a leader the 1979 Nicaraguan Revolution that toppled the US backed Somoza dictatorship that had held power for decades; and served as president from 1985 to 1990. In the US backed Contra Revolution financed by CIA drug trafficking and embargo that followed his election a right wing government gained power. Ortega's election victory gave him the presidency but not control of the National Assembly that is divided among four parties. Ortega's socialist policies are restrained but he is supported by Hugo Chavez of Venezuela and Evo Morales of Bolivia and his first act was to sign on to the Alternativa Bolivariana Party para las Americas (ALBA) an organization opposed to neo-liberal economics.

Countries that are members of ALBA include, Venezuela, Cuba, Bolivia, Nicaragua, and Ecuador. ALBA's objectives are based on principles of cooperation, solidarity, and mutual assistance; the goal is to create a new Bolivarian Republic, independent of outside interests. After being refused U.S. assistance to modernise the Nicaraguan Armed Forces to fight drug trafficking and organised crime Ortega asked for Russian assistance and received a quick positive response with a visit by a high level Russian delegation154.

The education of the people that began under Ortega and ended seventeen years ago with the US backed neo-liberal government has been reactivated with help coming from ALBA. On July 19th 2009 Nicaragua became the fourth Latin American country to be freed from illiteracy thanks to Cuban and Venezuelan technical, logistical, and financial support155.

Socialism in El Salvador

Maricio Fuenes who leads the Farabundo Marti National Liberation Front (FMLN) was elected on March 15 and inaugurated as president on the 1st of June 2009. Fuenes replaced the US backed neo-liberal government with its' paramilitary death squads that that murdered more than 75,000 people during the civil war that ended 17 years ago. There is real hope for democracy once again in El Salvador. The FMLN abandoned its' guerrilla war in 1992 and built a political opposition that finally prevailed156.

El Salvador was a typical liberal democracy before the left won the election where .03 percent of the population had 44% of the wealth and owned the media. There was no public broadcasting in El Salvador until 2004 when three young activists realised that the corporate media had been defeating any possibility of the left winning an election by running dirty campaigns smearing the opposition. Radio Zurda was the product of a radical youth media collective that now broadcasts weekly on 22 stations with a live internet feed in El Salvador. There are eight other allied organizations in El Salvador, Europe, and the U.S. who transmit their programs on the internet157. Radio Zurda broadcasts community and local news that is of interest to communities, and has acquired a large following158.

Socialism in Cuba,

Communism has been demonised by the US anywhere it has gained power, but nowhere has the demonisation been as vindictive and unrelenting, as against Cuba. China is still a Communist country and yet it has become the number one trading partner of the US and the EU. Despite facing a trade embargo by the US, and many western countries for decades the Cuban people have survived proud and free, and despite the poverty; they are much better educated than people in the US, enjoy universal health care, and no homelessness. Today few countries still boycott Cuba although the US persists.

Cubans were the first people in the Caribbean or Latin American countries to become educated, and receive universal health care, following their revolution in 1959. Cuba's Latin American School of Medicine currently provides 11,000 scholarships free of charge to students from dozens of countries; including 500 from the US, who wish to become MDs. In exchange students must pledge to practice medicine in an under served area in their home country. Cuba has the distinction of having the largest number of doctors per capita in the world, and has sent thousands of volunteer doctors, and medical staff, to serve in third world countries. To date Cuba has trained more than 78,000 doctors and reached out in solidarity to more than 100 countries throughout the world including the U.S.159. With the help of Venezuela they plan to graduate 100,000 more doctors during the next 15 years160. Currently, collaboration is being offered to 78 nations. Cubans live longer than almost anyone in Latin America, almost all of them have been vaccinated, and parasites, TB, malaria, and even HIV/AIDS are rare or non-existent161.

The United Nations, in December of 2008 recognized Cuba's contributions to health through The World and Pan-American Health Organizations (WHO/PAHO)162. The Cuban health care system is producing a population that is as healthy as the world's wealthiest countries at a fraction of the cost, and is exporting health care around the world to under served communities. More than 5000 foreigners travelled to Cuba in 2008 for medical treatment. Cuba is a world leader in the treatment of breast and neck cancer; and has licensed a German company with rights to produce their drug for the European market.

Cuba has also developed very advanced medical equipment that is sold internationally163, and has made many significant advances in medicine; the Finlay Institute in the West Havana scientific complex developed a vaccine 15 years ago to prevent meningococcal meningitis, and it remains the only vaccine of that type in the world. A Cuban vaccine for lung cancer is now being tested internationally for final approval for distribution to the public164; an amazing feat for an impoverished county living under a blockade.

Cuba has also made great contributions in the education of the people in other Latin American countries with Cuban teachers; Venezuela in 2006, and Bolivia in 2008, were the 2nd and 3rd Latin American countries to achieve fully educated populations, and Nicaragua is slated to be the fourth later in 2009. The Nicaraguan literacy campaign was dedicated to Fidel Castro in honour of development of the "Yes, I Can" program that is used by many international organisations, including the United Nations Educational, Scientific, and Cultural Organization.

Cuba has been praised by the UN as a world model for its' ability to feed its' people and the Cuban peoples right to food. Due to the US embargo food was often in short supply but it was always rationed so that everyone could eat. Cuba currently has a new program in the countryside aimed at making the country less dependent on food imports165. Even though food has often been in short supply it is shared and rationed and there are no food banks in Cuba.

Cuba's economy grew by only 4.3% in 2008 due to massive loses caused by 3 hurricanes that cost the country more than $10. billion dollars. For the past five years Cuba has been receiving more than two million visitors, and in 2008 saw an increase of 13.5% some 2.35 million visitors166. Cuba enjoys direct flights with 39 cities around the world, served by 94 scheduled and charter airlines. More than 110,000 workers are employed in Cuba's tourism industry; 41.22% are women, 57.24% have a high school education, and 20% are university graduates. Cubans are very hospitable people and make tourists feel very welcome. You will not find any beggars or panhandlers in Cuba; Cubans may be poor by our standards but they have great pride, generosity, and integrity. Tourism was Cuba's number two industry in 2008, second to the nickel industry.

Socialism in South America.

Democracy is contagious and so is the new socialism in South America. For those countries that have not yet turned left, turmoil, repression and protests are about all the Oligarchs have left to look forward to. Ecuadorian Indians are being repressed, beaten, and killed while attempting to protect their land from mining companies. In Peru in June 23 police and 10 Indians were killed in a protest to protect their land from oil, and mining projects. In Chile the largest Indian tribe is pushing for political autonomy and clashing with the government167. The drug wars, and war for liberation between various factions and the government in Columbia continue with murders and disappearances a daily occurrence. Even Brazil despite its' growing power and wealth still has a large landless organised group pushing for land. The word of the success of democracy in

Venezuela, and Bolivia has been spreading throughout Latin America since the people got their own satellite. The demands by the people for public and community media continue and Argentina recently revised its' broadcasting law to open up the airwaves to competition to the corporate monopoly.

Socialism in Europe.

Following the Second World War many countries that are now part of the European Union rewrote their constitutions and incorporated proportional representation into their electoral systems, and adopted many socialist programs. Proportional representation has provided these countries with better representative social democratic governments, often formed by coalitions. Free education that sent only the best scholars on through university has produced impressive results on all fronts, particularly the politicians it has produced. Germany rose from the ashes and destruction of war to become the most powerful economy in the EU.

Despite the pressures from Anglo Capitalists during the past thirty years, and reductions in Social programs, the people of France still enjoy many of the advances they achieved earlier such as a thirty four hour work week with benefits, and retirement at age fifty five. In a country with high unemployment such as France it makes sense, and it is also, necessary to shorten the work week so that more people can be employed to share the costs of social programs. France has remained the centre of the arts in the world because of its' social policies, that subsidise artists among other things. However, there is much more to French culture than social programs; the French still value family time together; houses instead of apartments, fresh locally grown food, fresh baked bread every day, and dinner is not a rushed affair on the run, it is a time to relax and spend time with family or friends.

A strong market economy still prevails in France, and fresh baked bread is available from small independent bakeries in every neighbourhood, not national bakeries supplying a preserved replica. Stores in France also are primarily independent and specialised, not huge chains of box stores that attempt to sell everything. Many products offered in French stores appear expensive compared to North America, but most of the products are produced in Europe and are of much higher quality.

The Baltic countries, Denmark, Sweden, and Norway are among the best places in the world to live according to the UN. While tax structures in many EU countries make it almost impossible for people to become billionaires, and the goal of egalitarianism is usually kept in perspective; Denmark lays claim to the largest per capita share of millionaires in the world. Denmark was also named the country with the most contented citizens in the world in 2008. This is similar to the position that Canada was in 40 years ago when Canada was rated number one in the world.

EU countries have not escaped the ravages of globalisation and cuts to social programs and deteriorating living conditions following in the wake of the US meltdown. Europeans in general are not accepting the cuts and strikes and protests are regular events in many countries. Greeks exploded in December 2008 after a fifteen year old boy was shot by police, and anarchy rocked Greece from the six of the month until the protesters stopped for Christmas. For eighteen days Greeks occupied universities, attacked police, police stations and banks. Damage in Athens alone has been estimated at one billion dollars. The shooting was a shot that reverberated around the world. As word spread, solidarity actions erupted in many EU countries, and people in more than fifty countries around the world acted in solidarity and held protests.

In France, "A report by the French domestic intelligence service talks of "a rebirth of the violent extreme left" across Europe that is likely to be aggravated by the effects of the economic crisis. Other secret documents expose alleged links with activists in Italy, Greece, Germany and the UK. "It has been growing for three or four years now and the violence is getting closer and closer to real terrorism," said Eric Dénécé, director of the French centre of intelligence research and a former Defence Ministry consultant." In January 2009 the French conducted a general strike that literally brought the country to a standstill for a day.

Europeans are fed up with cuts to their social programs and tax cuts for the wealthy and corporations. Most tellingly, the Scotsman newspaper drew attention to the response of French President Nicolas Sarkozy to the Greek events. Sarkozy rejecting budget proposals from his own party that he considered too obviously biased toward the wealthy, remarked, "Look what is going on in Greece." Sarkozy expressed concern that unrest could spread to France, the Scotsman reported that Sarkozy said:

> "The French people love it when I'm in a carriage with Carla, but at the same time they've guillotined a king,"

Perceptions of Socialism

Socialism has been portrayed in North America particularly the US as evil, akin to: Communism; however, programs such as public education, unemployment insurance, and social security pensions are all Socialist programs. In the mixed economies, of the G8, the US, is the only country without universal health care. Meanwhile the US has the most expensive health care in the world, and 45 or more million people with no health care; because their system is private for profit, and many people can not afford it. .In some countries public utilities, natural resources, and banks are also in the public sector, but this varies from one country to another.

Many Socialists believe in free enterprise, that Mercantilism is good for small businesses and small corporations, but that private for profit corporations must be prevented, from forming monopolies, and not be subsidised by taxpayers. The recent bailout of investment banks and mortgage companies in the US by the government is Socialism in reverse; and it is very ironic that in the US, Socialist practices are being used to aid the wealthy but not the people who will pay for the bailouts. The bank bailouts which were supposedly to generate liquidity in the domestic system, ironically ended up financing foreign investments, and continued multi million dollar bonuses for bank executives. The wealthiest 1% in the US hold more than 90% of the wealth already but they also want to control the wealth being generated by emerging economies so the people are being turned into serfs to pay for these grandiose plans.

Socialist governments help and protect the weakest members of society, and attempt to aid the progress of humanity; not create or maintain an elite class that lives off the labours of the rest. The only countries in the Caribbean, Central and South America that have educated all of their people and provide them with health care are socialist. Venezuela provided Cuba with oil in exchange for teachers and doctors. Venezuela provided London England with oil that benefited 250,000 poor people with half price transportation in exchange for advice from the mayor of London on how to govern cities. Cuba has provided many countries with doctors and medical teams often with no payment of any kind. In contrast, capitalism denies education and health care to those who can not afford to pay for it.

In North America we have been living under media dominated by corporate capitalist propaganda for decades and most of us really have no idea of what is really going on in the world. The New 21st Century Socialism that began ten years ago in Venezuela has been spreading rapidly in South America since the public has gained access to some media. Many European and British politicians have endorsed this new direct democracy, and have been greatly impressed by the benefits it has brought to the people. Many people believe that 21st Century Socialism is the only hope for a better future free from wars.

Chapter Seven

Democracy, Rights and Freedoms

"It is almost universally felt that when we call a country democratic we are praising it; consequently, the defenders of every kind of regime claim that it is a democracy, and fear that they might have to stop using the word if it was tied down to any one meaning."

George Orwell168.

Nothing has changed, there are many countries in the world today that claim to be democracies.

Communism, capitalism, socialism, and democracy.

Communism as it developed in Russia was state capitalism as opposed to private capitalism. In both state and private capitalism the population all work for wages. In Russia the state owned the natural resources, and means of production while in the US capitalists own the natural resources and means of production but in both cases the people work for wages.

Communism in China freed the slaves and serfs in the countryside and gave them their own land. The people in the cities were given a place to live and paid wages. The people in the countryside provided their surplus production to feed the city dwellers and in return received clothing and essential household goods. This was a mixture of capitalism and socialism providing wages to some and goods to the rest.

Neither, capitalism or communism were, or are democratic. China's government is officially a people's dictatorship; perhaps in their new socialism it may become more democratic as the government revises the party electoral system from the ground to the top, however it does not appear to have been very democratic in the past. There is no need for a two party, or multi party system in order to have a democracy by and for the people but democracy requires that everyone has a right to participate; and not just in the elections. As the level and quality of education in China improve we can expect to see changes at the local level that will gradually advance to the provincial and state governments.

The objective of the New 21st Century Socialism in Venezuela is direct democracy, real democracy, which has been absent from the world for more than two thousand years. When democracy was born in the ancient Greek cities states it was not difficult to call the population to a meeting and ultimately decide collectively who they wanted to lead them. After city states were incorporated into countries political parties arose and the people were duped into the notion that these parties would represent their wishes; representative "democracy" was born. The first two party system was devised by Italian Oligarchs in a city state long before the first revolutions to create the illusion of democracy while taking turns ruling and fleecing their sheep.

The means of achieving real democracy are dependent on the people forming communal groups from the local level, villages and towns, the countryside, public services, factories, cities, and provinces or states through to the national level. These communal groups elect representatives for a period of two years, but these representatives can be recalled at any time. Achieving democracy in the work place is achieved similarly by the workers taking over the means of production and continuing production with out bosses, owners, or shareholders. The management of each factory and the various jobs rotate among the workers and there is no privileged management class; eliminating the parasites in a capitalist society who do not work.

Democracy in the US.

The US does not have democracy and was never intended to have democracy. Democracy is not mentioned even once in the US constitution. Thomas Jefferson who wrote the Declaration of Independence and was the third president of the US said:

> "A democracy is nothing more than mob rule, where fifty-one percent of the people may take away the rights of the other forty-nine169."

There is certainly no danger of mob rule in the US where less than one percent of the population are taking away the rights of ninety-nine percent of the population. Why does the US claim that it is a democracy?

As George Orwell said:

> "It is almost universally felt that when we call a country democratic we are praising it; consequently, the defenders of every kind of regime claim that it is a democracy, and fear that they might have to stop using the word if it was tied down to any one meaning"170.

The word democracy comes from ancient Greece 4th and 5th century BC and means: "people rule, demos kpatoc"171. "A government by the people; especially: rule of the majority"172.

In a Capitalistic society there can be no democracy.

Albert Einstein wrote in 1949:

> "... capitalists inevitably control, directly or indirectly, the main sources of information (press, radio, education)173.

Democracy and freedom as touted to the world by the US have nothing to do with people; it is about the rights given to Corporations and Oligarchs to rape and pillage people and natural resources, not just in the US but throughout the world. In North America the vast majority of the population have watched their standard of living steadily decreasing since the 1970s, due to the deregulation of capitalism; this would have been impossible in a democracy where the people ruled.

The lack of democracy, in North America, that has permitted Corporations and Oligarchs to take control of our governments was a concern that Dwight D Eisenhower warned about, in his farewell address as the president.

"In the councils of government, we must guard against the acquisition of unwarranted influence, whether sought or unsought, by the military-industrial complex. The potential for the disastrous rise of misplaced power exists and will persist."

Dwight D. Eisenhower

Eisenhower went unheeded and the US military complex now consumes over fifty percent of the US, GNP; and is larger than the combined defence spending in the rest of the world combined. Expenditures such as this serve no other purpose than imperialism.

Democracy in Canada

Canada's government is based on the British Parliamentary system that was never intended to be democratic. The Canadian system has a senate and a House of Commons while the British system has a House of Lords and a House of Commons. The House of Lords in the British system originally ruled on all matters of importance particularly the spending of money that might be passed by the House of Commons; much like the power of the US senate over the House of Representatives. In the House of Lords in Britain Lords were appointed by the King, in Canada senators are appointed by the serving Prime Minister. After the second world war Canada followed many western countries into a social democracy because of the popularity of communism, and the winning of a provincial government in Saskatchewan by the socialist CCF party; and the CCF threat to the national election.

Canada's Support for Democracy

Canada's support for democracy for people is next to nil; social democracy has been dying a slow death under neo-liberalism. Canada's support for corporatacy can not be questioned.

Canada's involvement in Latin America provides conclusive proof that the Canadian government supports the worst human rights offenders and drug traffickers in the hemisphere, not democracy.

Canada's failure to call the coup in Honduras what it was, and failure to cut off military and foreign aid was a slap in the face for Canadians174,175.

Canada's signing of a free trade agreement with Columbia was akin to a pact with the devil. Columbia has the worst human rights record in the hemisphere.

As 2008 drew to a close five to six million families were homeless in the US, their unemployment rate may have been fifteen percent and still rising by more than half a million per month mid way through 2009. Food banks in the US were having trouble supplying needed food, there are demonstrations against the bank bailouts for the rich in many states despite the police repression. As inequality increased, crime increased, police forces grew, and taxes increased even more; the US already had the largest prison population on earth, and the un-safest streets. Washington DC has the dubious reputation of the murder capital of the world, and inequality in some US cities now rivals that of Africa. How can anyone claim that democracy exists in such a country?

Switzerland is credited by some with having the most democratic government in the world and has also been free of war for some five hundred years. Swiss freedom is attributed to their advanced form of representative democracy and a population that is trained for national defence. Prior to the 1990s the Swiss could mobilize over four hundred thousand armed men in a matter of hours; the militia keep their weapons at home. Switzerland has the best army for the money in the world due to a large well trained reserve force with up to date weapons, and a small professional army of officers and training staff. Switzerland's unique democracy limits the military budget, and the ability of the leaders to involve the country in a war of aggression. Switzerland has one of the highest rates of gun ownership in the world, and soldiers completing their term of service are permitted to keep their weapons.

Venezuela is the leading democracy in the Americas and the country is training and arming a large part of its' population with to protect their democracy, and defend their country against an invasion. Cuba trained its' people for self defence after the revolution for the same reasons as Switzerland; to make it extremely difficult for any invading force. Cuba was invaded only once soon after the revolution and quickly decimated the attacking mercenaries. Switzerland was the first country to train its people for self defence and it has served their country well. After serving their term of duty in the armed forces the Swiss people were given their weapons to take home with them. It is interesting to note in contrast that most western "democracies" have very strict gun controls, and untrained citizens.

Looking at the history of direct democracy since its conception in ancient Greece it appears that an educated public who can debate political issues and are also trained to defend their democracy are essential to preserve it. Direct democracy is only possible with an educated population that has the ability to intelligently discuss and debate political issues.

Why do North Americans continue to permit Corporate Democracy?

The perception that the majority of the people are doing well which was true several decades ago and the control of the media by corporations since then has perpetuated the myth and keeps the population divided by promoting friction between factions opposed to the government on issues such as; Natives rights, Women's rights, the Greens, gays, involvement in the wars, military spending, the poor, and crime and punishment. Until these groups can come together to form a united front against their oppressor, and common enemy, and develop their own independent media as some South American countries are doing, they will remain victims living in the dark in ignorance. People will continue being led to bash the poor, support cuts to social programs, and blame the poor for steadily increasing taxes that in reality only go to provide greater profits to corporations, and more wealth to the wealthy. Corporate media doesn't just sell needless products it has become the means of social control.

Corporate media seldom comes out with good news instead it concentrates on crime, violence, wars, and human rights abuses on other continents, not on ours; it vilifies Native peoples attempts to defend their land, unions as being responsible for uncompetitive business due to demands for decent wages and working conditions, environmentalists for obstructing corporations ability to exploit and pollute the environment, and the cost of social programs including health care, education and pensions because they are obstacles to greater corporate profits.

The single greatest obstacle to a peoples' democracy in South American countries has been the corporate media; although military coups are still possible as seen this year in Honduras. Hondurans lost their independent media and left without communications after the coup took over and only music or propaganda was permitted by the coup on the airwaves. Over the course of more than three months with a firm grip on the media, many of the leaders of opposition groups were arrested; many people were intimidated, beaten, killed, or disappeared in an attempt to bring the mass protests, blockades, and general strikes slowly to a halt.

But the coups' repression failed to work because some people have telephones and computers and the moccasin telegraph still works; it took awhile to start spreading the news and then the protests began to escalate week after week as the news spread.

What does Democracy really mean to the US and Canadian Governments?

While most of the world recognised that a military coup had taken place in Honduras, withdrew their ambassadors, and cut off foreign aid the US and Canadian governments didn't agree. A popular democratically elected president was kidnapped by the army at gun point in his pyjamas at 2 am in the morning and flown out of the country. Wasn't that a coup? In the following months both the US, and Canada held out for a mediated settlement with the coup regime while the UN, the EU, and the OAS demanded the presidents immediate return. The US action was regarded as a delaying tactic so that the coup could put down the popular mass rebellion that took place under a media blackout, and Canada was viewed as a US poodle. The purpose of the coup was to prevent the people from holding a referendum on the question of rewriting their constitution as the people of Venezuela and Bolivia had done.

As the coup in Honduras dragged on speculation that it was Obama's first coup gave way as the facts emerged proving that the US government had been behind the coup from the beginning. Some speculated that perhaps Obama had no control over the US government but as the president he is held responsible for what his government does. Three months later the popular protests had not been silenced as anticipated through violent repression, they had progressively grown stronger. U.S. and Canadian foreign aid helped preserve the coup regime from collapsing financially even though the EU had suspended financial aid immediately and many countries also suspended trade. Three months after the coup not one country in the world had extended recognition to the de facto government and most countries had withdrawn their ambassadors.

During the days and weeks that followed the coup protesters were killed, beaten, imprisoned, disappeared, and harassed by the army and police as they staged mass demonstrations, and general strikes demanding the return of their president, and or democracy. Zelaya wasn't as popular as his proposal to hold a referendum on re-writing the constitution which has huge support. The media blackout worked in North America, and Honduras but not in Latin America. Arrest warrants were issued for many of the legitimate elected representatives of the people, including the president, and various leaders of the populist groups that supported the government. Some of these people attempted to escape to El Salvador over the mountains because the army had set up roadblocks to prevent travel on the highways that left thousands stranded without food or water. A priest named Tamayo who was the leader of an environmental group protesting illegal logging on their land managed to escape an army attack in the middle of the night on the buses his group was traveling on; he went into hiding in fear for his life176. Prior to the coup Tamayo had been protected by guards from the army177. A month after the coup the president visited with many of his supporters who had escaped the army patrols and found refuge in Nicaragua178.

Honduran women were at the forefront of a lot of the resistance; and that fact alone would have caused uproar from the public in North America if they had known that women were being beaten, raped, and arrested for protesting179. However thanks to corporate media most people in North America heard nothing about these outrages. Honduran women's groups led by Gilda Rivera and more than 5,000 other activists occupied the National Institute of Women in protest of the appointment of a coup supporter as director of the organization. The coup appointed leader intended to reverse the gains that the women's groups had made in recent years posing serious threats to recently won rights. They took over the building to prevent the illegitimate government from pushing its program on women. Women were very prominent in the marches and blockades as well as can be seen in the many photos that have been posted by individuals, and independent media180,181.

To suppress information foreign news reporters were barred and all media was blocked off except that under the control of the coup; electricity and communications were also turned off to keep everyone in the dark. This made it difficult for the people of Honduras to find out what was going on and with the cooperation of most western corporate media few people in North America became aware of what was taking place either. As usual the best sources for news in English about events in the Americas were China, Cuba, and independent media in countries such as New Zealand, and Australia. US mass media has made no mention of the violence, killings, disappearances, and other human rights abuses in Honduras. US human rights groups that howl about China, and Cuba have also been curiously silent.

Independent media including Narconews provided some of the best in depth coverage on location, and Adrienne Pine publishing on quotha.net and several other web sites provided excellent research on who was behind the coup as well as publishing for a friend named "Oscar" who was on the scene. An interesting article written by Latinos in Fronteras in Los Angeles was published by Scoop in New Zealand. Ironically Scoop published several very informative articles on what was taking place in Honduras while almost nothing could be found on corporate North American news. UpsideDownWorld with writers from around the world, and a focus on Latin America also published several good reports

Canada was equally as guilty as the US in not opposing the coup, cutting off foreign aid and failing to tell the public what was going on182. Honduras is the largest recipient of Canadian foreign aid and military support in South America; and Canada's aid is second only to that of the US. Canadians know that that foreign aid comes from the taxes they pay; but most are not aware that Canadian corporations have huge stakes in Honduras that would be severely restricted in their mining and labour practices under an updated modern Honduran democratic constitution written by and for the people and this is the real reason for the foreign aid from Canadian taxpayers.

Considering that the president had already decided to cancel all future mining concessions in Honduras in 2006 long before he was kidnapped provides speculation about the Canadian government support for his removal183. People must begin to realize that the foreign aid comes from their taxes and is no different than payola to the powers that be for their co-operation with corporations for the benefit of capitalist investors. Few Canadians if they were aware would support their government's attempts to prevent democracy or support and subsidize what Canadian mining companies have been doing to the people and the environment in Honduras.

When a South or Central American country rewrites its' constitution in the hope of developing a new 21st century Socialism it is replacing a constitution that was imposed against the wishes of the people as most constitutions in the world have been. Most constitutions were written by and for the elites or in the case of South America often by military dictatorships and Oligarchs as in Honduras. In Venezuela, and Bolivia where new constitutions have been written by and for the people the indigenous peoples have been enabled with political rights and their cultures recognized; and all of the people at the community level have the right to decide what kind of economic development they will permit on their land. It is this direct democracy granted to the people in democratic constitutions that is most feared by neo-liberal "free" trade corporate governments.

As the people rise up in more countries demanding real democratic constitutions the oppression and repression is expected to increase or develop into a regional war against those countries that are developing real democracies. If the people of South and Central America are permitted to continue rewriting their constitutions and reforming their governments it will not only stop the looting and pillaging by foreign corporations it could also spread to North America. Many people in North America realize that they do not live in a democracy; they just do not know how to go about getting one. Gandhi led India to freedom from the British, and Martin Luther King freed Afro Americans from gross discrimination through peaceful protests; the same proven methods are being used to bring democracy to Latin American countries today.

The big difference in South and Central America is that many people are no longer illiterate, many people now have cell phones and internet access and there are increasingly more independent sources for news.

The coup in Honduras in June 2009, and the proliferation of US military bases in Columbia the following month demonstrate the lengths that Capitalists will go to in order to prevent democracy. The day of the coup Obama was credited with his first coup d'etat184. Columbia has one of the worst records in the world for human rights abuses, killings, and disappearances and the US has been supporting this "death squad democracy" in its forty year war against the people185.

Honduras is a classic banana republic producing bananas and pineapples for export controlled by mainly US corporations, Dole, Chiquita, and the United Fruit Company who supported the reign of terror186. Honduras served as a key US transportation hub to supply weapons to the Contras to overthrow the government of Nicaragua in the 1980s and ship cocaine back to the US to pay for them187. In 2006 Texaco and Shell were replaced as the suppliers of imported gasoline by other suppliers at lower prices188. Eva Golinger reported that Washington was behind the coup and offers proof in a report published by Global Research that is quite convincing189.

A large part of the population of Honduras were still marching and demonstrating against the coup more than four months after it began and the beatings, arrests, intimidation and targeting killings of leaders was still going on190. In mid October the coup was still intent on proceeding with a November election that many countries already said they would not recognize. The coup leaders say they are unconcerned about recognition perhaps confident that they do not need trade with other countries with the US and Canada continuing to finance them with foreign aid and train and supply their military.

The people of Latin America have learned that all groups opposed to their government must join together to protest to obtain change, and also to elect one of their own if and when an election opportunity presents itself; none of the traditional parties will allow the people to produce a new constitution if they can prevent it as has been made very clear by the coup in Honduras.

Neo-liberal "Free" trade agreements led to the destruction of the economies around the world; not just in South America. Iceland and Latvia have also experienced increased poverty, and the reduction or total elimination of many social services while their governments sunk deeper into debt. The same thing is taking place in Canada and the U.S., it just began later and is now beginning to become apparent to many people. It was these "free" trade agreements that led to the revolt by the people that resulted in the people rewriting their constitutions and bringing in real democracy to Bolivia and Venezuela.

What kind of democracy does the US support?

In South America it is the Columbian model where the US has contributed $6 billion dollars since the year 2000191, and that is expected to run to 10 billion under the new agreement.

What kind of democracy does Columbia have? Columbia has one of the worst human rights records in the world; the government spies on its leading citizens and Supreme Court judges who have also suffered intimidation; there is no end in site for its forty year war with dissidents, and has a government mired in controversy over corruption and working with paramilitaries that involves as many as 20% of the senators192. Uribe won fraudulent elections in 2002 to become president and since then has waged war on all opposition.193. Uribes' background and history has a great deal in common with Noriega of Panama194,195,196. Escobar touted by Forbes magazine as one of the richest men in the world was a Columbian drug lord in the cocaine trade who died mysteriously in 1993 and went on to become the personification in US pop culture only exhibited by the most criminally successful197. Columbian paramilitary death squads have been funded by US companies such as Chiquita for many years.198.

3,000 members of the Columbian army are currently under investigation by the justice system, and 27 officers including commanding General Mario Montoya were retired in disgrace following revelations that army troops had kidnapped poor young men from urban areas killed them and then claimed they were dead "guerrilla fighters"199. Popular protests are met with violent repression; a road blockade by some ten thousand people was attacked by the army with 2 killed and some 90 wounded, mostly by bullets while dispersing the demonstration200. During the six years of the current Uribe administration 1,243 natives have been killed and 54,000 displaced from their lands201. There is a demand by the people for the cancellation of the "free" trade agreement with the US that is rightly seen as an agreement "between owners and against the people", and a rejection of Plan Columbia.202.

Columbia has long been the number one drug producer in all of the Americas and this has not changed since the US started financing the drug war in Columbia; to the contrary there has been an increase in drug production203,204. Should we wonder why? "Hundreds of tons of Columbian cocaine, and to a lesser extent heroin, continue to flood into the US each year205".

On the other hand the price of opium in Afghanistan has dropped significantly206, despite a reduction in production. I wonder why? Opium production in Afghanistan had been nearly eliminated under the Taliban in 2001 according to the UN. Two years after the fall of the Taliban under the U.S. occupation production had increased tenfold surpassing Mujahadeen era levels207.

The current president Uribe has a long history of involvement in drug production and trafficking208,209,210. Uribe also leads a government that has had one fifth of its' senators convicted just in the past year of complicity with paramilitary death squad groups who silence opposition with intimidation and murder and then occupy native lands for drug production211. Journalists and human rights defenders are, and have been intimidated as well as the judiciary as human rights abuses continue to escalate212. "The UN High Commission for Refugees has the most work with internal refugees with over 4 million inside Columbia and a further million in Ecuador and Venezuela"213. Why does Columbia have the highest number of refugees? To put it simply Columbia has no democracy for the people. A former president of Columbia, Samper 1998-2002 had his visa to the US revoked for his connections to the Cali drug cartel who had donated $5 million to his election campaign. Uribe posted him to Paris as the Columbian ambassador until it provoked an upheaval in Columbia's diplomatic corps and he was replaced.214.

This is just a brief look at what kind of democracy the US supports; the whole story can be found by reading numerous articles that can be accessed through the endnotes.215. The US is currently planning to increase its support to Columbia by occupying five more military bases for a total of seven in Columbia along the Ecuadorian and Venezuelan borders and increasing funding.216. Uribe the president bypassed the Columbian senate in his agreement with the US who now say that he did not have the authority to sign the agreement.217. What do Columbians have to look forward to?

Perhaps the million Columbian refugees in Ecuador and Venezuela, particularly those in refugee camps near the borders of Ecuador and Venezuela can look forward to a blood bath like Panama; where thousands of civilians were killed during the US invasion in 1989.218. The Columbian people continue the fight in armed struggle because they have no other choice except extermination.219. It does not help the peoples' resistance that Bush labelled the FARC a terrorist organization and it also does make it true.

The Columbia resistance, FARC has been fighting for democracy and freedom for more than 40 years. 40,000 full time armed revolutionaries and 100,000 more in militia reserves continue the battle.220.

There is no question that a great deal of force will be required, and many people will have to die to suppress the demands for real democracy by the people who oppose "free" trade and corporatacy for government. This is a job for the paramilitaries because regular troops have problems with killing unarmed civilians especially women and children. The US had to turn to the use of paramilitaries such as Blackwater in Iraq for the same reason, and also the fact that it was becoming very difficult to recruit canon fodder for Iraq other than promising Latinos who would serve in the army US citizenship if they survived. The recruiting situation has changed recently with the mass unemployment created by the melt down.

"US policymakers continue to rank Columbia as vital to American national interests"221. Although there was much criticism by Pelosi and the democrats before Obama was elected it has since evaporated as have attempts to investigate 911.222. Like all of Obamas' election promises, were just the opposite is what has been taking place. There is no question that Columbia is vital to the interests of US corporations.223. The threat of ALBA spreading peoples' democracy from South America to the north keeps coming up in various news sources224. Who are the enemies of peace and democracy.225?

It has become obvious to the people in South America who their common enemy is: neo-liberalism, the IMF, U.S. "free" trade, globalization, foreign corporations, and the U.S. military.226. With people becoming educated and aware of corporate media propaganda it is unlikely that coups or corporate governments will survive in South America over the long run regardless of oppression, murders, and disappearances. The internet and new public media have spread the word that a better world is possible and it has already begun in Venezuela and Bolivia. Public radio stations and TV are being set up, as well as local community radio. Venezuela is setting up Peace Bases along the border and a newspaper to counter the US military build up in Columbia.227,228. Latin America has begun to look for economic and political independence and the heads of UNASUR the union of South American nations despite their countries differences are united and strongly condemn US military interference.229.

Rights and Freedoms

Cherished freedoms such as the right to bear arms in the US have nothing to do with Capitalism or Socialism; the right to bear arms was written into the US constitution, and could be written into the constitution of any country, be it Capitalist, Socialist, or Communist. It is interesting to note that the word democracy does not appear anywhere in the US constitution. Most developed and developing countries place restrictions of some sort, or ban the population from bearing arms. In view of the number of homicides in the US because of the gun laws perhaps some form of restriction is in order; however no peoples in the world want to be in the position of being unable to defend themselves against tyranny, or dictatorship.

Most of the citizens of Switzerland have military weapons in their homes courtesy of their government; they also have a very low crime rate because they enjoy a relatively egalitarian culture and live with a much more democratic form of government. The freedom to improve your situation in life, another cherished right in the US is enjoyed by all people who live in developed countries and many developing countries; and again has nothing to do with capitalism it is simply a matter of good economic principles. Trade in the form of mercantilism has been going on in the world for several thousand years permitting people to improve their situation in life.

Chapter Eight

Some final thoughts

There have been huge changes to the faces of capitalism and socialism since the Second World War. Perception of these changes varies greatly by most people born in each successive generation since then. However a record of the success and failures of the different economic and political ideologies exists and it should not be difficult for national leaders today to choose the best course for their people. That is, if they place the interests of their people first.

Since the meltdown got underway in 2008 China rose from the 4th largest economy to 2nd displacing Germany, and Japan. If the current trend continues China could displace the U.S. in two years. While most socialist countries have fared quite well through the melt down; countries following the neo-liberal model are suffering the most severe effects. As foreign trade shrank socialist countries like China, and Venezuela stimulated their economies by increasing social programs, diversifying trade, and building infrastructure to help the people while neo-liberal countries like the U.S., and Britain reduced social programs and put their people deeper in debt to bail out their bankers.

The visionary ideal of Simón Bolívar, who liberated South America from Spain; and the ideal of the new Bolivarian revolution that is underway in South America is to achieve.

"The most perfect system of government is that which produces the greatest sum of happiness possible, the greatest sum of social security and the greatest sum of political stability."

Simon Bolivar

Few people would argue against Bolivar's ideal but can we accomplish it? Capitalism reached its peak several decades ago with neo-liberalism and is now in freefall worldwide. Socialism has been reconceived for the 21st century and is making a comeback. This is a momentous time in the history of the world and great changes are taking place. Let us all hope that these changes will take place peacefully.

Endnotes

1   Enoch, Simon. Changing the Ideological Fabric? A Brief History of (Canadian) Neo-liberalism. http://www.stateofnature.org/changingTheIdeological.html.

2   Ibid.

3   Pachico, Elyssa. Rural Revolution in Columbia Goes Digital. http://upside downworld.org/main/content/view/2101/61/.

4   Chossudovsky, Michel. The Globalization of Poverty and the New World Order. http://globalresearch.ca/globaloutlook/GofP.html.

5   Terrorizing Dissent. http:///www.terrorizingdissent.org.

6   Adrian Croft. A Top Church of England bishop has told bankers those who speculate on falling share prices in the financial sector are "bank robbers". http://www.news.com.au/dailytelegraph/story/

7   Monkerud, Don. Wealth Inequality Destroys US ideals. http://globalresearch. ca/index.php?context+va&aid=14752. August 12th 2009.

8   Most Hungarians feel life was better under communism. Http://21century socialism.com/article/most_hungarians_feel_life_was_better_under_communism_01674.html June 6th 2008.

9   Julia Bonstein. Majority of Eastern Germans Feel Life Better under Communism. Der Spiegel 3rd July 2009.

10 Venezuela and Citgo Assure Continuity of US Heating oil program. http://www.venezuelanalysis.com/news/4090. January 7th, 2009.

11 Eva Golinger. Washington behind the Honduras coup: Here is the evidence. Global Research, July 15, 2009. chavezcode.com – 2009-07-13.

12 Cuban tourism growing despite world crises. Havana, May 8th 2009. http://wwww.gramma,cu/ingles/index,html

13 Venezuela Achievements of 10 Years Of Revolution. Ministry of Peoples Power for Communication and Information. January 30th 2009. http://www.venezuelanalysis.com

14 National Law Center on Homelessness and Poverty. http://www.pbs.org/now/shows/305/homelessness in the United States.

15 The National Center on Family Homelessness. CNN

16 Study: 7.3 million in U.S. prison system in '07 updates 3:09 p.m. EST, Mon March 2, 2009. http://www.cnn.com/2009/CRIME/03/02/record_prison_population/

17 UN Inequality in major US cities rivals Africa. Thursday October 23rd 2008. http://www.reuters.com/aricle/domesticNews/

18 A $5 Billion Bet on Better Education. http://www.nytimes.com/2009/08/24/us/24iht-letter.html

19 UN-Habitat. http://www.unhabitat.org/downloads/docs/global%20s.pdf

20 Parry, Robert. Why the Rights Propaganda Works. http:www.consortiumnews.com/2009/081809.html.

21 Upside Down World. Community Media in Times of Popular Struggle-fromVenezuela to Oaxaca to Honduras. http://upsidedownworld.org/main/content

22 http://www.capitalism.org/faq/capitalism.htm

23 Einstein "Why Socialism" Albert Einstein originally published in the first issue of Monthly Review (May 1949).

24 Marie Trigoma. Argentina's Soy Storm Tensions Rising Among Farmers, Monday 28 April, 2008. Towwardfreedom.com.

25 Noor, Jaisal. Worker Run Businesses Flourish in Argentina. (Indypendent) http://www.elcambiosilencioso.com.ar/?p=313. Agosto 14th, 2009.

26 Constitution of Venezuela. W http:///en.wikipedia.org//wiki/Constitution of Venezuela.

27 file://localhost/C:/Documents%20and%20Settings/John/My%20Documents/New%20Socialism/Anarchists/Anarchism%20-%20The%20logical%20structure%20-%20Introduction.mht

28 http://www.anarchy.no/

29 Selling sex legally in New Zealand. http://news.bbc.co.uk/2/hi/asia-pacific/7927461.stm

30 Swiss approve heroin program, Sunday November 30th, 2008, Canadian Press: The Associated Press.

31 Mark Stevenson. Mexico Decriminalizes Small Scale Drug Possession. http://www.huffingtonpost.com/2009/08/21/mexico-decriminalixes-sma n 264904.html.

32 Coucelman, Charlie. Canadian Senate Committee Recommends Legalizing Marijuana. 9/27/9002. http://media.guilfordian.com/media/storage/paper 281/.

33 The Contras, Cocaine, and Covert Operations. National Security Electronic Briefing Book No. 2. Http://www.gwu.edu/~nsarchiv/NSAEBB/NSAEBB2/nsaebb2.htm.

34 Fernandez, Belen. Honduras Reports Lack of Towns Named for Oliver North. The Narco News Bulletin, http://www.narconews.com/Issue59/article3777.html.

35 Afghanistan Opium and the Taliban. http://opioids.com/afghanistan/index.html. Feb 15, 2001.

36 Robichaud, Carl. Afghanistan's Latest Drug Report: The Hidden Story. http://www.tcf.org/list.asp?type=NC&pubid=979. The Century Foundation, 11,22/2004.

37 Ibid.

38 Soloman, Norman. Media Focus on CIS's Cocaine Links Is Long Overdue. Creators Syndicate. mediabeat@igc.apc.org.

39   http://www.suntimes.com/news
40   Almeida, Gregorio, J. Perez. The Controversial Secret Ingredient of Coco Cola. http://www.boliviasc.org.uk/index.php?option=com_content&task=view&id=27&Itemid=9.
41   Thornton, Mark. Alcohol Prohibition Was a Failure. July 17, 1991. Cato Institute. Policy Analysis no 157. http://www.cato.org/pub_display.php?pub_id1017.
42   Ibid.
43   Nadelmann, Ethan, A.. Let's End Drug Prohibition. http://online.wsj.com/article/SB122843683581681375.html.
44   http://www.ameinfo.com/157243.html.
45   Currency of the Khilafah Thursday, 17 July 2008 Abdul-Kareem
46   http://www.ameinfo.com/157243.html Growing Market
47   Safer Haven In the Financial Storm? http://news.sky.com/skynews/Home/UK-News/Islamic-Banking-And Finance----
48   Binladin Group raises $266mn with Islamic bond. http://www.arabianbusiness.com/531399-
49   Cecilia Valente. http://www.arabianbusiness.com/532095-deutsche-bank-to-launch-sharia-hedge-fund-range.
50   Condorcet "Sketch For A Historical Picture of The Progress Of The Human Mind" Weidenfeld And Nicolson London, 1795
51   51http://21stcenturysocialism.com/article/most_hungarians_feel_life_was_better_under_communism_01674.html
52   Gelder, Sarah van. Cuba Exports Better Health Care. Yes! Magazine. 5th June 2007. http://upsidedownworld.org/main/content/view/764/43/.
53   Lebowitz, Michael A.. The Path to Human Development: Capitalism or Socialism?. http://readingfromtheleft.com/PDF/SP/ThePath.pdf.
54   Einstein, Albert, Why Socialism?. http://www.monthlyreview.org/598einstein.php
55   Ibid.
56   Giordano, Al. Walter Cronkite's Legacy Was Not Objectivity but One of Honesty. Sept. 9, 2009. http://narcosphere.narconews.com/the field/3420/.
57   Einstein "Why Socialism"Albert Einstein originally published in the first issue of Monthly Review (May 1949). http://www.monthlyreview.org/
58   Enoch, Simon. Changing the Ideological Fabric? A Brief History of (Canadian) Neo-liberalism. http://www.stateofnature.org/changingTheIdeological.html.
59   Clarke, Tony. Silent Coup: Confronting the Big Business Takeover of Canada. Canadian Centre for Policy Alternatives. Jan 1997.
60   Ibid.
61   Ibid.
62   Dobbin, Murray. The Myth of the Good Corporate Citizen: Canada and Democracy in the Age of Globalization. 2003.
63   Enoch, Simon. Changing the Ideological Fabric? A Brief History of (Canadian) Neo-liberalism. http://www.stateofnature.org/changingTheIdeological.html
64   Ibed.

65 Ibed.

66 Ibed.

67 Ernst, Alan. From Liberal Continentalism to Neo-conservatism: North American Free Trade and the politics of the cd Howe institute. Studies in Political Economy. A Socialist Review. Number 39, autumn 1992, pp109-140. http://www.carleton.ca/spe/back-issues-archive.htm?select1-d39.

68 Enoch, Simon. Changing the Ideological Fabric? A Brief History of (Canadian) Neo-liberalism. http://www.stateofnature.org/changingTheIdeological.html

69 Written by Upside Down World . Community Media in Times of Popular Struggle- from Venezuela to Oaxaca to Honduras. http://upsidedownworld. org/main/content/view/2071/1/.

70 Serrano, Pascual. Del Orinoco, Correa. September 6th 2009. Chavez and Press Images. Translated by Sean Seymour-Jones for Venezuelanalysis.com. Source: Rebelion. http://www.venezuelanalysis.com/analysis/4774.

71 Solo, Toni. "The Observer." A Nicaraguan day out for genocides Boswells. http://www.tortillaconsal.com/observer_nicaragua.html.

72 Kozloff, Nicolas. Honduras: Latin America's Media Battle Continues. http:// www.venezuelanalysis.com/analysis/4579.

73 Solo, Toni. Isolated and discredited 2 – the US in Latin America. 14 July 2009. http://www.tortillaconsal.com/obama2.html.

74 Cook, Mark. Rerun in Honduras Coup pretext recycled from Brazil. http:// upsidedownworld.org/main/content/view/2102/68/.

75 Eric,SJ. Our Voice Radio Progresso Honduras. http://quotha.net/node/218.

76 Pine, Adrienne, Organizes paramilitary attacks begin in Honduras. http:// quotha.net/node292.

77 Salisbury, Steve. Columbia: Trade, Drugs, and the U.S. Congress. http://www. fpri.org/enotes/200705.salisbury.columbiacongress.html.

78 U.S. Intelligence. U. S. Intelligence Listed Columbian President Uribe Among Important Columbian Narco Traffickers in 1991. http://www.gwu. edu/~nsarchiv/NSAEBB/NSAEBB131/index.htm.

79 Bennett, Hans. A book review of. Blood and Capital by Jasmin Hristov. http:// upsidedownworld.org/main/content/view/2091/1/ . 3rd September 2009.

80 Leech, Gary. Anatomy of an Investigation: The Columbian States War Against Civil Society. http://columbiajournal.org/columbia303.htm. January 26, 2009.

81 Rivera, Carmen, Andrea. Behind the Headlines: Escobar's Hippo and the Calibio Battalion Columbia. http://upsidedownworld.org/main/content/ view/1995/61.

82 Corporate Plunder Watcher. Chiquita's hundred year history in Columbia. http://melbourne.indymedia.org/news/2007/06/146481.php.

83 Paley, Dawn. Deadly dealings around Canada-Columbia Free Trade Agreement. http://this.org/magazine/2009/08/24/canada-columbia-free-trade-agreement/.

84 McNulty, Caitlin, and Migliorelli, Liz. Media In Venezuela Facts and Fiction. http://upsidedownworld.org/main/content/view/2059/35/. 17 August 2009.

85   Chavez Hails Satellite Launch. http://www.venezuelanalysis.com/analysis/.
86   Ibid.
87   Ibid.
88   Ibid.
89   Cassel, Lainie. Avila TV in Venezuela: Revolutionizing Television. http://
     upsidedownworld.org/main/content/view/1904/35/. 11 June 2009.
90   Ibid.
91   Ibid.
92   British MPs commend Venezuelan democracy. January 1st 2008 http://21st
     centurysocialism.com/article/british_mps_commend_venezuelan_
     democracy_01593.html.
93   Serrano, Pascual. Del Orinoco, Correa. September 6th 2009. Chavez and Press
     Images. Translated by Sean Seymour-Jones for Venezuelanalysis.com. Source:
     Rebellion. http://www.venezuelanalysis.com/analysis/4774.
94   Dangl, Benjamin. Bolivia Looking Forward: New Constitution Passsed,
     Celebrations Hit the Streets. 26, Jan. 2009. http://www.counterpunch.org/
     dangl01272009.html.
95   Phillips, Peter. Socialism Seems to be Working in Venezuela. MinutemanMedia.
     org. Http://venezuelanalysis.com/analysis/4104.
96   Chossudovsky, Michel. The Globalization of Poverty. http://globalreseach.ca/
     globaloutlook/GofP.html.
97   A Massive Campaign On EI IS Needed. http://www.peoplesvoice.ca/
     articleprint33/03)_A_MASSIVE_CAMPAIGN_ON_EI_IS_NEEDED.html.
98   Bass, Frank, & Beamish, Rita. Banks that have their hands out in Washington
     this year were handing out multimillion-dollar rewards to their executives last
     year. The Associated Press. December 25, 2008.
99   McKenna, Barrie. In Wall Streets meltdown 5000 made a million. Washington-
     Globe and Mail Update. 30th July, 2009. 07:50 PM EDT.
100 Garcia, Oscar. Associated Press writer in Las Vegas for AP via Google News.
     Bailed Out Bank Execs in Vegas.
101 Clark, Andrew. In New York. Guardian.co.uk. Tuesday 10 February 2009
     15:34 GMT.
102 59 % of Canadians live payday to payday. http://www.cbc.ca/consumer/
     story/2009/09/14/payday-to-payday-problems.html.
103 The Canadian Press. Canada ties for last among developed countries for chills
     services: UNICEF. Wednesday, December 10, 2008\11:32 PM ET.
104 http://direct-democracy.geschichte-scheiz.ch/   Switzerland's   Direct
     Democracy.
105 Poland, John Lindsay. Yankees Go Home: U.S.s Unspoked Role in the Andean
     Conflict. Foreign Policy in Focus. March 7, 2008.
106 Oscar, translated by Adrienne Pine. Day 80, September 15 from Oscar. http://
     quotha.net/node/305.
107 Conroy, Bill. Race to expand U.S. military presence in Columbia draws yellow
     flag.. 15 September 2009 at 10:53 pm. http://narconews.com/.

108 Golinger, Eva. Washington behind the Honduras coup: Here is the evidence. Global Research, July 15, 2009. chavezcode.com – 2009-07-13.

109 Moore, Jennifer. Honduras: National Opposition To Coup Becomes A Social Force. 15 September 2009. http://upsidedownworld.org/main/content/view/2109/68/.

110 Conroy, Bill. Money talks in U.S. policy toward Honduran putsch regime. 13 September 2009 at 2:27 pm. http://narconews.com/.

111 Conroy, Bill and Giordano, Al. Pro Coupd Honduras Presidential Candidate Elvin Santos Is Key Beneficiary of Continued Government Funding. http://www.narconews.com/Issue59/article3766.html.

112 Military coups and US bases: The threat to Latin American democracy. http://www.greenleft.org.au/2009/808/41587.

113 Ibid.

114 Cregan, Fionuala. Argentina 50,000 March against Hunger. Wednesday, 17 December 2008. Fionuala_c@yahoo.co.uk.

115 Fionuala Cregan Wednesday, 17 December 2008

116 Trigoma, Marie. Argentine Factory Wins Legal Battle: FASINPAT Zanon Belongs to the People. http://upsidedownworld.org/main/content/view/2052/32/. 14 August 2009.

117 Weissman, Robert. Protests against neoliberalism IMF in Brazil, Coumbia. http://lists.essential.org/stop-imf/msg00210.html.

118 Ibid.

119 http://lists.essential.org/stop-imf/msg00210.html

120 Weissman, Robert. Protests against neoliberalism IMF in Brazil, Columbia. http://Lists.essential.org/stop-imf/msg00210.html.

121 Hallinan, Conn. Brazil Flexes Its' Muscles. http://www.counterpunch.org/hallinan099072009.html.

122 Ibid.

123 Michael Fox Wednesday, 28 January 2009

124 Rosset, Peter. Fixing our Global Food System, Food Sovereignty, and Redistributive Land Reform. http://monthlyreview.org/090817rosset.php.

125 Trigona, Marie. Argentina's Soy Storm Tensions Rising Among Farmers. 28 April 2008. TowardFreedom.com.

126 Howard, April. Saying No to Soy: The Campesino Struggle for Sustainable Agriculture in Paraguay. Upsidedownworld.org. april.m.howard@gmail.com.

127 Ibid.

128 Ibid.

129 Weisbrot, Mark. Neoliberalism Comes Unglued October 1998 http://www.zcommunications.org/zmzg/viewArticle/13530.

130 Castro, Fidel. Capitalism in Crises. Ocean Press, Australia. 2000. www.oceanpress.com.au.

131 Sudborough, Gary. Capitalism in Crises. http://seatle.indymedia.org/en/2008/11/270113.html.

132 BBC 26 Jan 09. Brokerage to pay Lehman investors.

133 http://mypage.uniserve.ca/~synergy/welcome.htm

134 http://www.reuters.com/article/domesticNews/idUSTRE49M7U220081023?
135 LeVine, Mark. A financial house of cards. http://english.aljazeera.net/focus/ outofwork/2009/02/200921712329491425.hmtl.
136 Martens, Pam. A Credit Crisis or a Collapsing Ponzi Scheme? 13 November 2008. Counterpunch. http://www.informationclearinghouse.info/article 21210.htm.
137 Monkerud, Don. Wealth Gap Will Widen in Downturn. http://www. zcommunications.org/zmag/viewArticle/22395. Sept. 2009.
138 Idid.
139 Democracy Now. Paraguay Rejects U.S. Military Deal. http://upsidedownworld. org/main/content/view/2114/68/.
140 European conference on Venezuela backs social reforms. November 14th 2007. http://21stcenturysocialism.com/article/european conference on venezuela backs radical social reforms 01571.html.
141 British MPs commend Venezuelan Democracy. Jan 1st 2008. http://21stcenturysocialism.com/article/british mps commend venezuelan democracy 01593.html.
142 British Parliamentary reception marks 10 years of Chavez. 21st Century Socialism. http://21stcenturysocialism.com/article/british parliamentary reception marks 10 years+of chavez.
143 Macdonald, Lisa. 2 August 2009. Imperialism: people power and solidarity. Green Left Weekly issue #805. August 5th 2009.
144 Sperling, Erik. Venezuelan Agricultural Production Has Grown, say Ranchers and Government. 12/12/2008. venezuelanalysis.com.
145 Ibid.
146 Suggett, James. Venezuelan Farmer Activists March Against Killings by Estate Owners. http://venezuelanalysis.com/news/4838.
147 Venezuelan Trade Declines with U.S., Increases with Brazil, Russia, China, and Japan. August 21, 2009. http://www.venezuelanalysis.com/
148 Pearson, Tamara. Communal Banks Of Venezuela Receive Big Boost. 14 November 2008. http://www.venezuelanalysis.com.
149 Dangl, Benjamin. Bolivia Looking Forward New Constitution Passed. http:// www.counterpunch.org/dangl01272009.html.
150 Ibid.
151 Ibid.
152 Denvir, Daniel. New Ecuadorian Constitution Approved by Strong Majority. http://caterwaulquarterly.com. 29 September 2008.
153 Ibid.
154 Jacobs, Karla. Recent news of important developments in Nicaragua. http:// www.tortillaconsal.com/nicaragua briefing.html. 6 August 2009.
155 Ibid.
156 Ramonet, Ignacio. The new South America. http://progreso-weekly.com/ index.php?option=com content&task=view&id=892&Itemid=1.

157 Thompson, Erica. Interview with Irma and Hubert Members of El Salvador's Radio Zurda. Friday 26th June 2009. http:://upsidedownworld.org/main/view/1926/74/.

158 Ibid.

159 More than 78,000 doctors trained in Cuba have worked in 100 countries in the world. http://www.cubascoop.com/cubascoop%20ingles/2008/08-12-15-More.html.

160 Gelder, Sarah van. Cuba Exports Better Healthcare. http://www.yesmagazine.org/issues/latin-america-rising/1733.

161 Gelder, Sarah van. Cuba Exports Better Healthcare. http://www.yesmagazine.org/issues/latin-america-rising/1733.

162 United Nations Recognizes Cuba's Medical Training. http://embacu.cubaminrex.cu/Default.aspx?tabid=13635.

163 Riera, Lilliam. Cuba exports medical equipment all over the world. http://www.gramma.cu/ingles/2008/enero/vier18/4indmed.html.

164 Padrino, Iris Armas. Cuba registers therapeutic vaccine for lung cancer. http://www.gramma.cu/ingles/2008/junio/mier25/27vacuna-i-html.

165 Replacing imports strategic objective for Cuba. http://cuba-1.umn.edu/?nid=64769.

166 Cuba tourism reached record levels in 2008. http://www.usatoday.com/travel/destinations/2009-01-13-cuba-record-tourism_N.htm.

167 Ecuador Indians clash with police. Oct. 1st http://english.aljazeera.net/news/americas/2009/10/20091014122145939.html.

168 Orwell, George. http://www.quotationspage.com/quotes/George_Orwell/

169 Jefferson, Thomas. Thomas Jefferson On Politics & Government. http://etext.virginia.edu/jefferson/quotations/

170 Orwell, George. http://www.quotationspage.com/quotes/George_Orwell/

171 Democracy. http://en.wikipedia.org/wiki/Democracy.

172 Democracy http:www.meriam-webster.com/dictionary/democracy.

173 Einstein Albert. "Why Socialism" Albert Einstein originally published in the first issue of Monthly Review (May 1949). http://www.monthlyreview.org/598einstein.php.

174 Holly, Ashley. Canada Supports the Military Coup in Honduras. Global Research, July 14th 2009.

175 Ditchburn, Jennifer. Canada upholds military aid program with Honduras despite coup. The Canadian Press.http://news.therecord.com/printArticle/577899. related articles. Xinhau, Tico Times.

176 Sanchis, Eva. Exclusive Priest Fears Fur His Life After Coup In Honduras. El Diario/La Prensa. News Report. Translated by Elena Shore, Posted: July 02, 2009.

177 Ibed.

178 Supporters cross border to back Zelaya. Xinhau. July 27 2009. Xinhau News Agency July 28, 2009.

179 USW Women of Steel Ask Lawmakers to Protect Honduran Women Brutalized by Coup Regime. Mom, 08/31/2009. AP http://assets.usw.org/Releases/wos to Clinton honduras 6 pdf.

180 Lovato, Roberto. Honduran Women at Forefront of Resistance to Coup. New America Media, Interview. July 22, 2009.

181 Carlson, Laura. Coup Catalyses Honduran Women's Movement. http://www.pacificfreepress.com/news/1/4576-coup-catalyzes-honduran-womens-movement.html.

182 Holly, Ashley. Canada Supports the Military Coup in Honduras. Global Research, July 14, 2009. TheTyee.ca-2009-07-09.

183 Ibid

184 Golinger, Eva. Obama's First Coup d'Etat: Honduran President has been Kidnapped: Updates 1-17. http://www.venezuelanalysis.com/analysis/4554.

185 Rozoff, Rick. US Escalates War Plans In Latin America. Columbia: Forty Year War. http://www.globalresearh.ca/index.php?context=va&aid=14503.

186 186Corporate plunder watcher. Chiquitas hundred year history in Columbia. http://melbourne,indymedia.org/news/2007/06/14681.php.

187 Fernandez, Belen. Honduras Reports Lack of Towns Named for Oliver North. The Narco News Bulletin, http://www.narconews.com/Issue59/article3777.html.

188 Fernandez, Belen. Juan and Pedro Enter the Honduras Oil Import Business; Coup d'Etat Follows. http://narconews.com/Issue59/article3779.html.

189 Golinger, Eva. Washington behind the Honfuras coup: Here is the evidence. July 15 2009. http://www.globalresearch.ca/index.php?context=va&aid=14390.

190 Pine, Adrienne. Continued political assassinations in Honduras. August 2009. http://quotha.net/node/257.

191 Sojo Julianna. Council on Hemispheric Affairs. Ten Years of Plan Columbia: Bogota Leases Military Real Estate to the Obama Administration. 5th August 2009.

192 Isacson, Adam. Columbia's imperiled democracy. http://www.opendemocracy.net/article/columbias-imperilled-democracy. 6/03/2009..

193 Columbia: Is a negotiated solution possible? http://latinamericasolidarity.org/2009/04/20/columbia-is-a-negotiated-solution-possible?. http://latinamericasolidarity.org/2009/04/20/columbia

194 Rowlands, David, t. Panama Twenty years on from US invasion. Green Left Weekly issue #808 26 August 2009.

195 Boron, Atilio. Uribe in the Mirror. http://alainet.org/active/32661&lang=eng.

196 National Security Archives. http://www.gwu.edu/~nsarchiv/NSAEBB/NSFAEBB131/dial910923.pdf.

197 Rivera, Carmen Andrea. Behind the Headlines Escobars Hippo and the Calibio Battalion Columbia. 16 July 2009. La Raza Chronicles. KPFA, 94.1 FM.

198 Salisbury, Steve. Columbia: Trade Drugs and the US Congress. http://www.fpri.org/enotes/200705.salisbury.columbiacongress.html. May 2007.

199 Zibechi, Raul. Columbia: Social Conflict Replaces Warfare. Americas Policy Program, Center for International Policy. (CIP). 11th December 2008.

200 Ibed

201 Ibed

202 Ibed

203 Columbia: Is a negotiated solution possible? http://latinamericasolidarity. org/2009/04/20/columbia-is-a-negotiated-solution-possible?

204 Diaz, Nidia. A sharp retort to US military intervention. http://www.gramma. cu/ingles/2009/septiembre/mier3/UNASUR.html.

205 Salisbury, Steve. Columbia: Trade Drugs and the US Congress. http://www. fpri.org/enotes/200705.salisbury.columbiacongress.html. May 2007.

206 UN. Afghan opium market in decline. http://www.cbc.ca/world/ story/2009/09/02/afghanistan-opium-un-survey382.html#soacialcomments.

207 Robichaud, Carl. Afghanistans Latest Drug Report: The Hidden Story. The Century Foundationn, 11/22/2004. http://www.tcf.org/list.asp?type=NC& pubid=979.

208 Ibed

209 Molinski, Dan. US Intelligence Listed Columbian President Uribe Among Important Columbian Narco Traffickers In 1991. www.gwu.edu/-nsarchiv/ NSAEBB/NSAEBB131/index.htm

210 Salisbury, Steve. Columbia: Trade Drugs and the US Congress. http://www. fpri.org/enotes/200705.salisbury.columbiacongress.html. May 2007.

211 Columbia: Is a negotiated solution possible? http://latinamericasolidarity. org/2009/04/20/columbia-is-a-negotiated-solution-possible?

212 Smyth, Frank. Uribe courts hold critical journalists in contempt. http://www. cpj.org/blog/2009/03/uribe-columbian-courts-hold-critical-jounalists-i.php.

213 Ibed.

214 Uribe in Columbia diplomats row. http://news.bbc.co.uk/2/hi/americas/ 5173048.stm.

215 Rowlands, David, t. Panama Twenty years on from US invasion. Green Left Weekly issue #808 26 August 2009.

216 Planas, Roque. U.S. bases Stoke the Flames of Regional Conflict. Aug. 19th 2009. NACLA. http://www.venezuelanalysis.com/analtsis/4730.

217 Ibid.

218 Rowlands, David T. Panama: Twenty years on from US invasion. http://www. greenleft.org.au/2009/808/41543.

219 Isacson, Adam, The Columbia-Venexuela-Ecuador tangle. 14 March 2008. in, Pearce, Jeremy. Columbia: who are the enemies of peace and democracy? http://www.opendemocracy.net/article/democracy power/politics protest/ Columbia peace and democracy enemies. 9-04-2008.

220 Columbia: Is a negotiated solution possible? http://latinamericasolidarity. org/2009/04/20/columbia-is-a-negotiated-solution-possible?. http://latin americasolidarity.org/2009/04/20/columbia.

221 Salisbury, Steve. Columbia: Trade Drugs and the US Congress. http://www. fpri.org/enotes/200705.salisbury.columbiacongress.html. May 2007.

222 Ibed.

223 Ibed.

224 Ibed.

225 Pearce, Jeremy. Columbia: who are the enemies of peace and democracy? http://www.opendemocracy.net/article/democracy_power/politics_protest/ Columbia_peace_and_democracy_enemies. 9-04-2008.

226 Rowlands, David, t. Panama Twenty years on from US invasion. Green Left Weekly issue #808 26 August 2009. http://www.greenleft.org. au/2009/808/41543

227 Suggett, James. Peace Bases to Counter U. S. Military Buildup in Columbia with Bi-national Reconciliation. August 28th 2009. http://www.venezuelanalysis. com/.

228 Pearson, Tamara. New National Progressive Newspaper Goes to Print in Venezuela.. September 2nd 2009. http://www.venezuelanalysis.com/news /4762.

229 Diaz, Nidia. A sharp retort to US military intervention. http://www.gramma. cu/ingles/2009/septiembre/mier3/UNASUR.html.